W9-BZP-398

When *Saints*
Sing *the* Blues

Other books by Brenda Poinsett

Celebrations That Touch the Heart
Not My Will but Thine
*Reaching Heaven: Discovering the Cornerstone of Jesus'
  Prayer Life*
She Walked with Jesus
Understanding a Woman's Depression
What Will I Do with the Rest of My Life?
When Jesus Prayed
*Why Do I Feel This Way? What Every Woman Needs to
  Know about Depression*

When *Saints* Sing *the* Blues

Understanding Depression *through the* Lives *of* Job, Naomi, Paul, *and* Others

Brenda Poinsett

BakerBooks
Grand Rapids, Michigan

© 2006 by Brenda Poinsett

Published by Baker Books
a division of Baker Publishing Group
P.O. Box 6287, Grand Rapids, MI 49516-6287
www.bakerbooks.com

Printed in the United States of America

Library of Congress Cataloging-in-Publication Data
Poinsett, Brenda.
    When Saints sing the blues : understanding depression through the lives of Job, Naomi, Paul, and others / Brenda Poinsett.
        p.   cm.
    Includes bibliographical references.
    ISBN 10: 0-8010-6570-4 (pbk.)
    ISBN 978-0-8010-6570-5 (pbk.)
    1. Depressed persons—Religious life. 2. Depression, Mental—Religious aspects—Christianity. 3. Bible—Biography. I. Title.
    BV4910.34.P65 2006
    248.8′625—dc22   2006003900

To
Bob, Ben,
and Christophe,
with whom I share
my home and my heart

Contents

Acknowledgments

Many thanks to Vicki Crumpton, senior acquisitions editor at Baker Publishing Group, for encouraging writers to share book ideas. Over dinner at her expense, we talked about several ideas, including one I called "When Saints Sing the Blues." She responded with the words that excite every writer's ears: "I want to hear more." I'm grateful she encouraged me to write a biblically based book on depression; it is a project I've seen a need for and wanted to do for a very long time.

Thanks also to the small Sunday-night group at First Baptist Church of St. Clair, Missouri, who graciously allowed me to explore the lives of some of the characters in *When Saints Sing the Blues*. With their help, I could get my feet wet and try out some of my interpretations, before perhaps embarrassing myself in print.

The church group was my initial sounding board, followed by my husband, Bob Poinsett, as I continued to work on the book. He read and critiqued each chapter, some of them several times. And he did it all without insisting on being listed as the coauthor! He and our son Ben were both

9

patient with me and encouraging as I maintained a tight writing schedule. I appreciate their flexibility and help.

Several people prayed for me, some faithfully and continually, others at various times. I'm grateful to Mary Rose Fox, Barbara Williams, Vi Burton, Myrna Turner, Jan Turner, Debbie Hawkins, Carileen Bollinger, Vivian McCaughan, Lorraine Powers, Susan Miller, Beulah Peoples, Janet Hofer, Chris Dulworth, Pat Townsend, Jim Poinsett, and Joel Poinsett. Others might have prayed too, and I failed to make note of it. I'm sorry and trust you will know that you pleased God and had a part in this project.

Gratitude also goes to Barbara Williams for some help with my grandson, Christophe, during vacation Bible school, so I could have some extra writing time. My sisters, Judy and Linda, and my brother, Myrle, were also considerate of my time by not demanding as much of me as they could have in looking after our dear mother.

Thanks also to Kenneth Steffen, Ministry by Mail coordinator of Roberts Library, who provided me with helpful resources about some giants of the faith who struggled with depression.

I don't know whether any of these people I've acknowledged ever sang the blues, but I do know they have helped me write a biblically based book for those who do. It was a group project, and I prefer it that way because I've learned like Moses the wisdom of sharing the spirit and sharing the load.

Introduction

I'm a Christian and I've known some blue times.

One time I was so down that I wanted to quit marching—just give up on life and serving God. I was down in a valley, and the hill ahead just looked too steep to climb.

Whenever I talk about that struggle, well-meaning Christians often question me about what my life was like at the time. I explain that I was an earnest, active Christian and a Sunday school teacher. I had a regular devotional life. I was a strong student of the Bible, an ardent pray-er, and an earnest follower of Christ.

In the silence that follows, I hear their unspoken questions: How could someone like you become depressed? How could a born-again, Bible-believing, faith-teaching, regular pray-er become depressed?

I understand. Sincere faith, Bible study, prayer, and commitment—all of these things are supposed to serve us well. These things are supposed to protect a person, to keep him or her from being sad and hopeless. We could understand if someone who was not doing these things

11

became depressed, but how could a Christian serving the Lord become depressed?

That's the question I want to answer in this book, and I'll do this by going to the Bible, our sourcebook and authority for living.

A Biblical Look

You won't find the words *depressed* and *depression* in the King James Version of the Bible or in the early manuscripts of the Bible. The word *depression* was first used in 1660 to describe low spirits and didn't come into wide use until the mid-nineteenth century,[1] but the symptoms are there. I recognize them because I've studied depression. Once I learned the blues were going to be a problem for me, I tried to learn all I could so I could help myself. What I discovered was so powerful I began sharing what I learned with others. I found eleven biblical characters who experienced depression:

Moses
Naomi
Job
Hannah
Saul
Elijah
Jeremiah
Jonah
Solomon
A psalmist
Paul

These people weren't depressed all the time, but along life's road, they encountered a dip, a time in a valley where visibility wasn't sharp and clear. It was as if rain clouds hovered overhead, and the sun didn't shine. It became difficult to travel on, and in their misery, they expressed honestly what they felt—sometimes to others but mostly to God. Each, in his or her own way, sang the blues.

If you have ever felt like singing the blues, then I invite you to look with me at the lives of these eleven people. Because we are believers, we need a biblical perspective.

For the Encouragement

Recently I put a note in our church newsletter about a new class on biblical characters who experienced depression. A church member called me as soon as she read it. She said, "I cried when I read your announcement."

Now all writers want people to be moved by what they write, but cry over an announcement? I had to ask, "Well, why?"

"I struggle with depression, and I thought I must be awful or weird. It's just such a relief to know that I am not the only one."

She had experienced the stigma associated with depression and had learned that strong people, especially believers, shouldn't ever be depressed. Part of the explanation for this may come from our oversimplification of the Christian life. In our motivational speeches, our sermons, our lessons, our articles—and, yes, our books!—we make life seem so simple. Just follow the six or ten or twenty easy principles and you will live happily ever after. Even when we allow for Satan's temptations, few speak of how difficult life itself can be or how challenging serving God really is.

We seem to think that Christians should be impervious to the hurts and trials of life, that whatever comes our way, no matter the magnitude, we should just accept it, thank the Lord, and keep on marching. And Christian leaders? Well, they should have the spiritual resources to handle whatever challenges come up. After all, they are to be our examples.

So if heartaches come to us or we get road weary from being a leader and we become depressed, no wonder we think we are awful or weird. We think we've failed as a Christian or that we're losers. We mutter to ourselves about how weak we are and surmise that something is really wrong with us. We fear we have lost favor with God or that he is disappointed in us. If that's the way you feel, then take heart, my friend, because our look at the biblical characters in the valleys of despair will show that you are in good company.

All eleven of these people were strong individuals, most were capable leaders, some were stellar in character, and all were valuable to God's ongoing purposes. Certainly nothing was inferior about any of them! As for weird, Jeremiah may have appeared a bit so at times, but he wasn't ever a bad person. He was a courageous person whom God used at a very crucial time in the life of his people.

We will see that, considering what they experienced, their singing the blues was a natural response to life's difficulties and challenges. We all have our load limits, and some of us respond by getting depressed. This may be a natural response, but that doesn't make it a pleasant one. Being in a dark valley is no fun. So how can you avoid going there? Why do some believers walk there and others don't? And once there, how do you get out? Some experts have some simple answers to these questions, which is another reason believers need a biblical look at depression.

The Spiritual Side of Depression

More and more often these days depression is seen as strictly a medical problem. I was shocked when I read in a book by a prominent, nationally known pastor that depression was not a particularly spiritual issue. He said it was a medical condition caused by many factors, including chemical imbalances in the brain.

The one good thing about this view is that it takes away the stigma associated with depression. The depressed person can say, "I have a chemical imbalance." Enough said. No one is going to ask him or her, "How could someone like you be depressed?"

But to define depression as strictly a chemical or medical problem ignores the fact that we are more than physical creatures. We are also spiritual, mental, emotional, and social creatures. Depression can enter our lives in any one of these areas, fan out, and affect other areas.

While depression may start as a mental problem, an emotional one, or a physical one, such as a chemical imbalance, it is going to affect our spirit. Hopelessness is a hallmark of depression. Many feel alienated from God, as if he abandoned them. Some feel they have lost their salvation. Some are disappointed at how God acted—or didn't act—in their lives, or they become disillusioned by something they were taught about God or faith. So no matter what the initial cause, depression will usually have some spiritual ramifications.

The primary cause of depression can also be spiritual (and then it would fan out to touch us physically, mentally, and emotionally). In my case, I probably wouldn't have become depressed if I hadn't been a Christian. My depression had its beginning in disappointment with God's leadership. Earnest prayer, I discovered, could not protect me from failure and defeat. Interwoven with the disappointment and perplexity was rejection by other Christians. The threads of depression were tightened by unexpressed anger over flippant responses to my pain and anxiety over our future. After some of the anxiousness subsided, I mulled over all that had happened and concluded that God did not have a purpose for my life. Without a purpose, I could see no point to getting up in the morning, and I found myself in a slough of despondency.

Believers need a biblical look at depression so we can understand the spiritual dynamics of what happens to us—how our spirit might be affected by the events of our life or what kinds of things can attack our spirit and bring on the blues.

The prophet Isaiah acknowledged the possibility of dark times in our lives. He said, "All of you that honor the Lord and obey the words of his servant, the path you walk may be dark indeed, but trust in the Lord, rely on your God" (Isa. 50:10). We want to trust in the Lord and rely on him to lead us out of the valley, but how? Here's where a case study approach—a look at the lives of biblical characters—is really valuable. What was involved in their depressions? And more important, how did they cope and eventually emerge from the valley?

About each biblical character, we will answer these questions:

- Who was the person?
- What were his or her circumstances that caused depression?
- What were the symptoms?
- How did the person deal with the circumstances?
- How did God respond?

- What can we learn from the person's efforts and God's responses?

Not all eleven people displayed the same symptoms and not all eleven dealt with their blues in the same way. We can't, for example, study the life of Moses and then say, "We know everything we need to know about depression." Depression has many causes and comes in many guises, and fortunately there are also many solutions!

While depression makes you feel hopeless, you aren't. Any general book on depression can give you help and hope for healing, but in this book we're going to look for biblical solutions. Christians want and need biblical answers, and by studying the lives of eleven biblical characters who were depressed, we can find those answers.

This is not to say that medical help is not important. To recover, to climb out of the valley, some of us will need medical help, but even then we may still need some spiritual insight to grow and gain from the experience. Yes, that's right, growth from depression is possible. I count it as one of the best things to ever happen to me. My struggle and subsequent recovery was a time of real growth for me, and the same can be true for you.

Learning from the Dark Times

The darkness of the valley is scary, and we don't want to dwell there, and yet our experience in the valley can be a valuable time of learning. We can sort out our theology, claim what we really believe, and discard what is wishful thinking. We can grow up in the faith. We can learn things about ourselves—who we are and what our strengths and weaknesses are. I know I am a much stronger person because of my experience with depression. I learned I have choices. I've developed a healthier lifestyle. I learned I had faulty thinking patterns, and I continue to work on changing those. I learned the importance of expressing my emotions and finding healthy ways to do it. I've had to exercise my faith muscle and stretch beyond where I would have ever gone on my own. The most important lesson I learned is that I need a purpose—a God-given purpose that connects me with eternity. I need a purpose that makes sense out of the nonsense of life, makes the humdrum and tedious palatable, gets me to look beyond the disappointments of life, and gives significance to what I do.

Leslie D. Weatherhead once referred to these kinds of gains as "treasures of darkness."

> Like all men, I love and prefer the sunny uplands of experience, when health, happiness, and success abound, but I have learned far more about God, life, and myself in the darkness of fear and failure than I have ever learned in the sunshine. There are such things as the treasures of darkness. The darkness, thank God, passes. *But what one learns in the darkness, one possesses forever.*[2]

There is no valley of depression so deep that God cannot bring gain out of it, but we may not know that unless we take a look at the lives of biblical characters who walked for a time in valleys of darkness. Come, walk in those valleys with me, and see what treasures God may have for you.

1

⊰| Moses |⊱

When the Load's Too Heavy

I can't be responsible for all these
people by myself, it's too much for me!

NUMBERS 11:14

*E*very time I packed clothes, food, toys, and soft drinks
for our family of five to take a vacation, I thought
of Moses. How did he ever move a caravan of six hundred
thousand men plus women and children with all their pos-
sessions through desert areas infested by hostile tribes? We
were traveling Midwestern highways in a station wagon,
and that was daunting enough!

God called Moses to take the Israelites to the land he
had promised them. At the time they were slaves in Egypt,
and their workload was intolerable. They cried out to God
for a deliverer, and he sent them Moses.

CEO of the Exodus

Moses bravely began his role by confronting the Egyptian pharaoh to seek the release of the Israelites. Naturally the pharaoh didn't want to let such a large workforce leave, so he resisted. God sent a number of plagues that changed his mind.

As the exodus got underway, the Israelites followed Moses toward the Promised Land. God directed their path with a pillar of cloud by day and a pillar of fire by night. After several days, they reached the Red Sea. Meanwhile, Pharaoh changed his mind about letting the Israelites go. He ordered his army to pursue them and bring them back. When the Israelites saw the army coming, they were terrified. They said to Moses, "Was it because there were no graves in Egypt that you brought us to the desert to die? What have you done to us by bringing us out of Egypt?" (Exod. 14:11 NIV).

Moses said, "Do not be afraid. Stand firm and you will see the deliverance the LORD will bring you today" (v. 13 NIV). And they did! The cloud that had been leading them moved to the back of the camp, hiding the Israelites from the Egyptians. A strong east wind blew all night and rolled back the waters of the sea. Awed by the sight, the Israelites rushed across the path in the sea. Following them in hot pursuit, the Egyptians raced out across the sea floor where the wheels of their chariots got clogged in the sand. They tried to turn back, but the wind stopped, and the receding water engulfed the Egyptian army. The Israelites were safe!

What a relief! What a sight to behold! What a trust-building experience! "When the Israelites saw the great power the LORD displayed against the Egyptians, the people feared the LORD and put their trust in him and in Moses his servant" (v. 31 NIV).

With a dramatic rescue like that, so indelibly imprinted on the minds of God's people, you would think that forever after they would be perfectly obedient to God and follow unquestionably Moses' leadership. The Bible, though, tells a different story. They complained, rebelled, and generally caused Moses grief until he was a person who could truly sing, "Nobody knows the trouble I've seen."

The "Troubles" He Saw

The complaints, rebellions, and protests of the Israelites added weight after weight to what Moses was already carrying, making his load heavier and heavier.

What are we to drink? From the Red Sea, the Israelites marched across the desert. After several days, water was hard to find. When they found some, the water was bitter. Forgetting they worshiped the God who parted the Red Sea, they hit the panic button and grumbled against Moses. "'Must we die of thirst?' they demanded" (Exod. 15:24 TLB).

What are we to eat? After being on their journey a month and a half, they wanted meat. Their lives weren't in danger, but they acted as if they were. They said to Moses, "If only we had died by the LORD's hand in Egypt! There we sat around pots of meat and ate all the food we wanted, but you have brought us out into this desert to starve this entire assembly to death" (16:3 NIV).

Is the Lord going to take care of us or not? On another occasion, when there was no water, "they grumbled against Moses. They said, 'Why did you bring us up out of Egypt to make us and our children and livestock die of thirst?'"

(17:3 NIV). Their fury was so great they were ready to stone Moses.

Who will protect us? As if providing for the physical needs of more than six hundred thousand people and keeping them headed in the right direction wasn't enough responsibility, Moses also had to be alert to attacks from other nations along the way. At Rephidim, the Amalekites attacked them. To counterattack, Moses commanded Joshua to draft able-bodied men to fight back.

Who will hear us? Moses spent his days hearing the people's complaints against each other, deciding what was right and wrong, and giving them wise solutions. When his father-in-law, Jethro, visited the camp, he saw what was happening and how much of Moses' time and energy was being consumed by the people. He said to Moses, "What you are doing is not good. . . . The work is too heavy for you; you cannot handle it alone" (18:17–18 NIV).

Give us a god we can see. When the Israelites reached the Desert of Sinai, they camped by a mountain where God gave them the Ten Commandments and other laws to govern them. A covenant was made between them. The people promised God, "All that you have said, we will do," which included not worshiping any other gods.

Their commitment didn't last long. When Moses left them to meet God on Mount Sinai, the people became restless. They forgot God; they forgot the laws he had given them. They built a golden calf—a tangible god—to worship.

We've had so many misfortunes. After the Israelites had been at Sinai for more than a year, they resumed their traveling. The covenant had been contracted, the law had been given, a tabernacle had been erected, and priests had been set apart. The people were developing into a distinctive nation, ready to settle in the Promised Land, but three days out, the people started complaining. To do so now after covenanting with God made their sin doubly grievous. God sent fire among them as a punishment, which ceased only after Moses pleaded with God on their behalf.

Moses, faithful and dependable, held on through difficult and frustrating circumstances that would have sunk many a leader. Through all the difficulties with God's people, Moses was generally patient and loving. He was a mighty pray-er and interceded on their behalf. Unlike the people, he did not forget about God's mighty power and trusted God to help them. God showed him how to find water for everyone to drink. God provided food for them. Quails came up and covered the ground. Manna (small seeds or thin flakes that could be made into flat cakes) was waiting for them each morning.

When they were fighting the Amalekites, Moses stood on top of the hill with the rod of God in his hand to give the people confidence. As long as the Israelites could see Moses with the rod upraised, they trusted God and had the courage to fight.

At times Moses became exasperated with the people, as he did when they wanted to stone him because there was no water. He wondered aloud to God, "What am I to do with these people?" At times he got angry with them, as he did when he saw the golden calf. He wondered how they could forget God and his commandments so soon.

Moses didn't become depressed, though, until a bluebird lighted on top of the load he was carrying. The toll of the stressful events and the leadership demands accumulated until Moses reached his load limit—something everyone has.

One Bluebird Too Many

My husband illustrates talks he gives with a cartoon he saw once in a magazine. The first frame of the cartoon shows a bridge with a sign on the side reading, "Load Limit: 8 Tons." The next frame shows a sand truck approaching the bridge. On the side of the truck is a sign showing the truck's weight, "8 Tons." The third frame shows the truck starting across the bridge and a bluebird flying down toward the truck in pursuit of a free ride. The final frame shows the bluebird landing on the truck now in the middle of the bridge, and the bridge collapsing. The bridge could support eight tons, but not eight tons and one bluebird!

Actually, most bridges will stand up under their posted limit and probably a few bluebirds extra, but all bridges have their breaking point. When the load becomes more than the bridge can sustain, it will collapse.

Like bridges, we too have our load limits. Some of us have higher limits of what we can carry than others, but we all have a point at which we may collapse under the pressure of weight added to our load. Some people may never reach their load limit, because they don't experience many stressful events or conditions in their lives. Others of us will, and it may just be the touch of one bluebird that causes us to break down.

You're on an airplane returning home after yet another high-pressured business trip. The airline attendant accidentally spills coffee on you, which means you will have to have your suit cleaned when you get home—one more detail to take care of. You smile at the attendant and tell her, "That's all right," but inside you fume, *Why wasn't she more careful? As clumsy as she is, how can she keep her job?* When your spouse meets you at baggage claim, your first words are, "I've had it. I can't do this anymore."

Or maybe you have been an active church member, always there every time the door is open. You teach Sunday school, serve as a greeter, serve on numerous committees, and lead mission trips to other countries. People marvel at your energy and hard work. And then one day, after an important meeting where food was served, you are left alone to do all the cleanup, and it is particularly messy. As you are mopping up spilled coffee, some junior highers run through the room and deliberately overturn your mop bucket. As their laughter fades down the hall, you think, *Those punks. They don't respect anything or anybody.* You decide, *I quit. I'm not cleaning up anymore around here or planning any more trips.* Eventually people start noticing your withdrawal and ask, "Are you all right?" You answer, "Sure, I'm fine," but inside you are not. You are depressed.

Now the depression of these two individuals was not caused by the spilled coffee or the mocking junior highers. It isn't the bluebird that breaks down a bridge, it's the eight tons already there that break down the bridge!

The day Moses became depressed, the people weren't in crisis. They were complaining again, but it wasn't a new complaint; but this time, it was too much for Moses. He had reached his load limit.

The Bluebird Lands

The grumbling started with the foreigners traveling with the Israelites. The foreigners were tired of the daily supply of bland manna. They wanted some chewy meat, crunchy vegetables, and flavorfully spiced foods. As they recalled the tasty meat and fish they had had in Egypt where they could have all they wanted, they activated the memories of the Israelites. Then the Israelites too began to complain.

"In Egypt we used to eat all the fish we wanted, and it cost us nothing. Remember the cucumbers, the watermelons, the leeks, the onions, and the garlic we had? But now our strength is gone. There is nothing at all to eat—nothing but this manna day after day!" (Num. 11:5–6).

They had forgotten how hard they had worked to have food to eat. They forgot the brick kilns, the taskmasters, and the sting of the whip. All the people stood around their tent entrances weeping and complaining. What an uproar that must have been, and sensitive Moses heard it all. God heard it too. He "became exceedingly angry" (v. 10 NIV).

The people's whining and complaining chipped away at Moses' already depleted energy. He had guided them out of Egypt, out of slavery; he had sustained his own faith even when theirs faltered; he had led the people to Sinai and helped them become a covenant people; he had withstood their constant griping and kept going. But now he was caught between complaining, uncooperative people on one hand and an angry God on the other, and Moses lost his cool.

Moses' Honest Prayer

Moses said to the Lord:

Why have you treated me so badly? Why are you displeased with me? Why have you given me the responsibility for all these people? I didn't create them or bring them to birth! Why should you ask me to act like a nurse and carry them in my arms like babies all the way to the land you promised to their ancestors? Where could I get enough meat for all these people? They keep whining and asking for meat. I can't be responsible for all these people by myself; it's too much for me! If you are going to treat me like this, have pity on me and kill me, so that I won't have to endure your cruelty any longer.

Numbers 11:11–15

Moses took his complaints to the Lord just as he had taken the complaints of the people to him on so many occasions. And it is in his honest prayer that we see the symptoms of his depression.

- Moses asked to die. He said, "Have pity on me and kill me" (v. 15). He was so fed up with the cantankerous behavior of the people and their continual complaining that death was a welcome thought. Wanting to die is a symptom of severe depression.

- Even though he mentioned their whining, he didn't blame the people. In his prayer, he blamed God. He was starkly honest as he made God responsible for his misery: "Why have *you* treated me so badly? Why are *you* displeased with me? Why have *you* given me the responsibility for all these people?" (v. 11, italics added).

- He felt sorry for himself. Depression is usually laced with self-pity. The tone of Moses' prayer is "what have I done to deserve this?" He said, "I didn't create them or bring them to birth! Why should *you* ask me to act like a nurse and carry them in my arms like babies all the way to the land you promised to their ancestors?" (v. 12, italics added).

- He saw the situation as impossible: "Where could I get enough meat for all these people? . . . I can't be responsible for all these people by myself; it's too much for me!" (vv. 13–14). Moses felt hopeless although he had experienced God's miraculous intervention all along just the way the people had.

- He experienced intense inner turmoil. Depressed people feel a particular kind of inner torment that is hard for other people to understand. Moses called it "wretchedness" (v. 15 KJV, RSV, AMP). He felt worthless, as if he had failed in everything he had done.

Moses' prayer not only shows his symptoms of depression but it shows us one good way of dealing with depression. He prayed honestly, expressing his feelings to God.

The Value of Honest Praying

What is honest praying? Isn't all praying honest? Well, yes, it is in the sense that it's impossible to lie to God. On the other hand, we can keep things covered up when we pray. We can do perfunctory prayers and never get real or specific. We can say the same prayer over and over until it becomes a meaningless rote activity in which we never really engage the self. We can pray about some things that need attention, such as the needs of others, and still leave a part of ourselves sealed off, untouched, and ignored.

Others are not quite honest in a different way, as if they have to dress up their prayers and speak in a special language to God; they don't feel they can be themselves. They think God wants to hear only about certain things, so they pray lofty prayers and don't mention what's really bothering them. God, they assume, doesn't want to be bothered. They have never learned that God is the only being who does not have a load limit. He is the only person on whom we can cast all of our cares (1 Peter 5:7).

28

So when I use the term "honest praying," which I'll use often in this book, I mean coming to God as you are, speaking in a language natural for you, letting God know how you feel and what's on your mind and in your heart.

Honest praying is valuable. It opens our wills to God, giving him the channel he needs to respond. If we hold back, we limit what God can do. When we pray honestly, we open up our inner space where God has room to work. This is important for those struggling with depression to know because "wretchedness" is on the inside, taking up space where God could be working.

Clogged inner space, where the damage of accumulated stress resides, affects our ability to hear. We may have difficulty receiving wisdom from others or hearing God speak. With honest praying we release the tension, allowing it to escape, and our hearing improves. If Moses had been stubborn and withheld how he felt, he might not have been able to hear God's solution to his dilemma. God had a remedy for his despair.

Share the Spirit and Share the Load

In response to Moses' honest prayer, God said to him, "Assemble seventy respected men who are recognized as leaders of the people, bring them to me at the Tent of my presence. . . . I will come down and speak with you there, and I will take some of the spirit I have given you and give it to them. Then they can help you bear the responsibility for these people, and you will not have to bear it alone" (Num. 11:16–17).

What sweet words those must have been to Moses! He would no longer have to carry the huge burden alone. Seventy elders would guide and lead the people along with

Moses, thus lifting some of the weight off his lonely shoulders. Plus they would be an encouragement to him as they shared his spirit, enthusiasm, and dedication.

Why hadn't Moses thought of sharing the spirit and sharing the load? Had he forgotten the advice his father-in-law, Jethro, had given him earlier? When Jethro noticed how the people's complaints were consuming Moses' time and energy, he told him to select good people to help him.

Though he applied Jethro's advice *at the time*, perhaps Moses simply forgot the advice as he continued to lead the Israelites. Continuing to change geographic locations and deal with cantankerous people would have challenged any system of organization. Perhaps Moses lapsed in overseeing his assistants. He may have found it difficult to delegate responsibility and share the workload. Many people do, even dynamic leaders. I've read where delegating work to others is one of the hardest time-management principles to practice, even though it is the sensible thing to do.

Or the consuming nature of continuous stress may have made Moses forget Jethro's advice. During ongoing, intense stress, such as he was experiencing, thinking can become cluttered. A friend described it as being in a snowstorm where the snow is blowing all around and visibility is poor. You do what you can to keep moving forward but you are never sure you are walking in the right direction. Now after his honest prayer, Moses knew what direction to take, even if he wasn't completely back to his old self.

Heading in the Right Direction

Moses readily gathered seventy elders for God to speak to and divvy up the load, but Moses had trouble processing another part of God's answer. God directed Moses to tell the people to get ready, because he was going to give them enough meat to last a whole month.

"Moses said to the Lord, 'Here I am leading 600,000 people, and you say that you will give them enough meat for a month? Could enough cattle and sheep be killed to satisfy them? Are all the fish in the sea enough for them?'" (Num. 11:21–22). While he had witnessed many miracles, the depression had dulled his ability to believe. Even when we sense a decisive moment has occurred in which we are better, we still may have some residue to deal with before we can be completely well. Recovery is a process, and fortunately for Moses, God was going to give him some dramatic evidence to remind him who he was.

The Lord said to Moses, "Is there a limit to my power? . . . You will soon see whether what I have said will happen or not!" (v. 23).

God sent a wind that brought quails from the sea. The people caught the quails and ate so many they became ill. He gave them what they were asking for, thus bringing them to see how foolish they were to despise the sufficient food he provided for them.

It wasn't long, then, until Moses was back being the strong leader that he had been. His depression had been a temporary dip. The snow flurries ceased, and he could clearly see the road ahead. With others sharing his spirit and sharing the load, he successfully led the people to the Promised Land. This didn't mean he became a perfect leader, but he did return to being a strong, faithful leader so that he became known as Israel's greatest prophet.

Replay and Reflect

What kind of load are you carrying?

How do complaining people affect you? Is complaining contagious?

Why are some people reluctant to pray honestly?

What is the value of honest praying?

Why is sharing our workload difficult?

How does a person share his or her spirit?

2

ᴥ| Naomi |ᴥ

When Bitterness Develops

The LORD's hand has gone out against
me!

RUTH 1:13 NIV

Although depression can occur without an apparent cause, most depressions are triggered by something. In Moses' story, we saw how accumulated stress was the cause. Now, in Naomi's story, we'll see how accumulated loss made her despondent.

Beginning with a Move

Naomi's name means "pleasant," a word that describes her nature and her life. She was a kind, thoughtful woman who enjoyed her family and friends. She lived a couple of hundred years after Moses. By now, the Israelites were living in the Promised Land, although they weren't unified as a nation and didn't have a king.

Naomi and her husband, Elimelech, along with their sons, Mahlon and Kilion, lived in Bethlehem of Judah. "Judah occupied a rugged plateau in the semiarid lands west of the Dead Sea. Normally, the land was fertile enough to sustain fields of wheat and barley, grape vineyards and groves of olive and fig trees. But occasionally the rains failed, the crops withered and there was famine."[1] During one such disaster, Naomi, Elimelech, and their sons left Judah and went to Moab, a kingdom on the east side of the Dead Sea. With the move, Naomi lost her home and more.

When we move to a new location, we lose more than a place of shelter and a geographic location. We lose the familiar, the sense of knowing where things are and whom we can trust. In Moab, Naomi and her family would not be trusted; they would be suspect. The Moabites and the people of Judah hated each other. No warm welcome awaited Naomi and her family. She would no longer be surrounded by God's people because the Moabites worshiped Chemosh and not the God of the Israelites. She would lose the opportunity to worship with those who believed in the same God she did and who practiced religion in the same way.

When we move, we also lose important connections—friends and family. Even though we determine we will stay in touch, eventually the distance grows between us. For Naomi, living in a time without cars, a postal system, or telephones, staying in touch with those back in Bethlehem would have been almost impossible. So when she lost her home, she also lost her friends and extended family.

Still, Naomi considered herself fortunate. The move was difficult, but she had Elimelech, Mahlon, and Kilion.

Moving meant food; it meant survival for her family! She counted herself blessed because she had an intact family where love abounded, support was given, and worship was unified, so she was optimistic about the future. She had no idea it would include more losses.

Loss upon Loss

Elimelech died. Naomi lost her husband and the father of her children. The loss was so painful she felt as if she had been split in half, forever maimed. As she grieved the loss of her husband, she was glad she had her two sons. They would be there to comfort her, to be her companions, and to support her.

Mahlon and Kilion married Moabite women, Ruth and Orpah. Naomi may have resisted at first their marrying Moabite women. If they had still been living in Bethlehem, they would have married Israelites. She did, though, welcome the companionship of the women and looked forward to the time when she would have grandchildren. What joy would fill the house!

Before long, though, the sons died. One simple phrase in the Bible describes Naomi's situation: "the woman was bereft" (Ruth 1:5 RSV). Her life now had a huge void in it; it felt empty and hollow. The loves of her life were gone.

Naomi coped the best she could. Her grief was exacerbated by one very large problem: How was she going to support herself?

Widows were to be provided for by their sons. This was not a time of equal employment opportunity for women or Social Security benefits for widows. In fact there were hardly any ways a woman could provide for herself. Women were dependent on men for economic and physical survival.

When Elimelech died, Naomi still had sons who would provide for her. With their deaths, she lost important relationships and financial support. What was she going to do?

News from Home

Naomi heard that the Lord had blessed his people back in Bethlehem. The famine was over. She still had relatives and friends there with whom she could reconnect, so she decided to return home. At first, she planned to take her daughters-in-law with her. The three would travel together facing whatever dangers they might encounter. This distance wasn't so long that it couldn't be walked in four or five days, but lawlessness reigned. It was a time when people did what was right in their own eyes (see Judges 17:6; 21:25; Ruth 1:1a). Who knew what they would encounter?

But Naomi saw that returning to Bethlehem was the best choice. As the three started out, Naomi must have remembered how hard it was for her to leave her home and move to a strange land. She also thought of the future of Ruth and Orpah. They would want to remarry and have children, and she knew it would be highly unlikely that any Israelites would want to marry Moabite women. She had grown to love her daughters-in-law and wanted them to have husbands and children, so she said, "Go back, each of you, to your mother's home. May the LORD show kindness to you, as you have shown to your dead and to me. May the LORD grant that each of you will find rest in the home of another husband" (Ruth 1:8–9 NIV).

Naomi kissed them good-bye. The decision was made. Then Orpah and Ruth started crying. They "said to her, 'No! We will go with you to your people'" (v. 10).

As heart wrenching as this moment must have been for her, Naomi unselfishly insisted they return home.

Naomi said, "Return home, my daughters. Why would you come with me? Am I going to have more sons, who could become your husbands? Return home, my daughters; I am too old to have another husband. Even if I thought there was still hope for me—even if I had a husband tonight and then gave birth to sons—would you wait until they grew up? Would you remain unmarried for them? No, my daughters. It is more bitter for me than for you, because the LORD's hand has gone out against me!"

verses 11–13 NIV

You may be scratching your head and saying, "Huh?" at Naomi's words about having sons that would grow up and marry Orpah and Ruth. Naomi was thinking of the Mosaic law that if a widow (in this case Orpah or Ruth) had no son but could still bear children, the deceased husband's brother was supposed to produce a son with her (Deut. 25:5–10). This would guarantee the continuation of the family name and property.

Naomi's mention of having more sons who would grow up to marry Ruth and Orpah was probably her way of exaggerating their circumstances to encourage the women to return home. She was thinking of them and not of herself. This doesn't mean that all was well with Naomi. Though she had been courageous, decisive, unselfish, and strong, these words to her daughters-in-law hint that she was hurting.

As she tried to help Ruth and Orpah see the impossibility of her finding husbands for them, she was pessimistic about her own situation. She said, "Even if I thought there was still hope for me," implying pessimism about her own future (Ruth 1:12 NIV). She also said she was bitter because "the LORD's hand has gone out against me!" (v. 13 NIV).

Ruth insisted on staying with Naomi. She clung to Naomi and committed herself to her. Orpah chose to stay in Moab.

Even though Naomi wanted Orpah to stay, and had encouraged her to, still that was another loss for Naomi. She had come to regard her daughters-in-law as daughters (see v. 3). This fresh loss may have set her to thinking as she and Ruth walked to Bethlehem.

Sojourn of Sorrow

Most people have a habitual style of dealing with what happens. For example, some people have a style of distracting themselves when trouble strikes. Another style is ruminating or chewing over what you have experienced.

The word *ruminating* means "chewing the cud." Animals, such as cattle, sheep, and goats, chew a cud composed of regurgitated, partially digested food. They chew it over and over. Ruminators do something similar with their thoughts. They hold up what's happened to them and view it from every angle. They make interpretations and continually revisit their conclusions. They try to figure out what happened and why.

This is not to say that ruminating is a bad characteristic. On the contrary, it can be a tremendous asset for students of the Bible, for news analysts, problem solvers, and philosophers. But it can be detrimental to someone like Naomi who had suffered many losses and whose future looked bleak.

We have no way of knowing if Naomi was a ruminator but we do know the walk back to Bethlehem would have provided a prime opportunity for it. Since Ruth and Naomi knew each other well, there wasn't a need for continuous conversation. They had long stretches where the silence was comfortable between them and there were few distractions along the roadway. Both women could be alone with their thoughts and possibly ruminate.

As Naomi retraced the route that she, Elimelech, Mahlon, and Kilion had walked years earlier, memories came flooding back of a simpler, happier time when all they had to worry about was food. She missed them so much and had lost so much. It was hard not to count the cost of all she had been through. She had lost her home, not once but twice. She had lost her husband and her sons. She had lost a daughter-in-law. All these were tangible losses that would affect anyone's spirit. But there were other things too, intangible things, things hard to talk about but things that could easily have occupied her thoughts. There was the loss of the familiar when she changed homes. There was the loss of confidence in the goodness of God.

And what about grandchildren? Her sons had been married for ten years but they had produced no children. Now she probably would never have any grandchildren. There would be nothing of her family to extend into the future. To the Israelites, "producing offspring assured a tangible afterlife, not just for yourself but for your entire family. Children were not a personal choice. They were the extension of one's whole clan into the future."[2]

The losses—tangible and intangible—stacked up, and her thoughts rolled around over and over in her mind as she and Ruth trudged their way to Bethlehem. By the time they arrived, sadness engulfed her.

Naomi's Depression

Not all people respond to loss with depression. You can grieve and be sad without experiencing depression, but for many people, even strong women like Naomi, it can be a problem when the losses stack up. And Naomi's grief was laced with anxiety, adding to her emotional turmoil. Not only did Naomi have to deal with the past, she had to think about the future too, and it held little promise for two widows.

As she and Ruth neared Bethlehem, Naomi became painfully aware of who she used to be and what her life had once been. Memories flooded her mind and fueled her ruminating.

"When they arrived, the whole town became excited, and the women there exclaimed, 'Is this really Naomi?'" (Ruth 1:19).

"'Don't call me Naomi,' she told them. 'Call me Mara, because the Almighty has made my life very bitter. I went away full, but the Lord has brought me back empty. Why call me Naomi? The Lord has afflicted me; the Almighty has brought misfortune upon me'"(vv. 20–21 NIV).

Naomi's description of her sojourn of sorrow reveals symptoms of depression:

Bitterness. When she spoke to her old friends, she said she didn't want to be called Naomi anymore. *Pleasant* was not a word that could describe her any longer. She suggested that Mara would be a better name for her because it meant bitterness.

Hopelessness. As noted above, she didn't see any probable solutions for her daughter-in-law or herself.

Feeling mistreated by God. Naomi blamed God for her sad life. Naomi said, "The Lord has turned against me" (v. 13), and "the Lord Almighty has condemned me and sent me trouble" (v. 21).

Cognitive distortion. The kind of ruminating response that leads to depression usually contains distorted thoughts, often of a pessimistic or negative nature. These thoughts are so automatic, a person may not be aware he or she is having them or how they are influencing feelings. Naomi's thinking wasn't quite accurate as evidenced by her comment to her friends, "When I left here, I had *plenty*, but the Lord has brought me back *without a thing*" (v. 21, italics added). When she left Bethlehem she had a lot—a husband, a connection with people, and faith—but she did not have food. A famine was in the land, so she did not have *plenty*. When she arrived back in Bethlehem, she was not "without a thing." She had a strong daughter-in-law and dear friend, Ruth, who would prove to be a tremendous asset to her.

Stuck in a holding pattern. While I have never heard anyone use the term *paralysis* with regard to depression, depressed people seem to be nearly paralyzed. Hopeless and pessimistic, many shut down as if there is nothing they can do. Though Naomi had the big problem looming before her of how two widows were going to provide for themselves, she did not take any action or suggest that Ruth take action. The decisiveness she exhibited when she left Moab seemed to have disappeared. Ruth was the one who took action.

Ruth to the Rescue

The harvest was beginning, so Ruth said to Naomi, "Let me go to the fields to gather the grain that the harvest workers leave" (Ruth 2:2). She was certain she could find some man who would let her glean in his field. By law, widows, orphans, and strangers were supposed to be allowed to pick up and keep the grain overlooked or dropped by the harvesters. This wouldn't be a long-term solution for Ruth and Naomi, but it would get them by so they wouldn't starve.

The field in which Ruth found herself working belonged to Boaz, a rich and influential man who was from the same clan as Elimelech. As she moved through the field picking up grain, Boaz noticed her. He asked his harvesters about her. The foreman told him who she was, how she cared for Naomi, and what a hard worker she was. Boaz was impressed. He told the harvesters to protect her and leave extra grain for her to collect.

Later, when Boaz spoke to Ruth, he gave her special instructions about gleaning and blessed her. He said, "May the LORD repay you for what you have done. May you be richly rewarded by the LORD, the God of Israel, under whose wings you have come to take refuge" (v. 12 NIV).

So Ruth gathered grain in the field until evening, and when she had beaten it out, she found she had nearly twenty-five pounds. She took the grain back into town and showed Naomi how much she had gathered.

Naomi's interest was piqued. She asked Ruth, "Where did you gather all this grain today? Whose field have you been working in? May God bless the man who took an interest in you!" (v. 19).

Did you notice that exclamation mark? Naomi's mood was starting to change.

Ruth told Naomi that she had been working in a field belonging to Boaz. Naomi's mood brightened even more, and the wheels of her mind started turning in a positive direction. *If Boaz, who was a relative, took an interest in Ruth, then perhaps he could be her kinsman-redeemer.*

The hope of an Israelite widow was that the nearest of kin to her dead husband would take her as his wife. If they had a son, that son would take the name of the former husband. In this way the dead man's family would continue (Deut. 25:5–10). Individuals who performed this duty were called kinsmen-redeemers. A kinsman-redeemer was also expected to look after helpless family members and redeem family property that had been lost through debts or some misfortune.

Hope rose within Naomi, chasing her blues away. With this boost, she realized that God wasn't against them as she had been thinking. She exclaimed to Ruth, "The Lord always keeps his promises to the living and the dead" (Ruth 2:20).

Ruth continued gleaning in the fields while Naomi did some serious thinking. This time, though, instead of pessimistic thoughts like the ones she brooded about on the road from Moab to Bethlehem, these were stimulating, mood-elevating thoughts as she pondered how to get Boaz to assume the role of kinsman-redeemer. There was something she could do to change their situation!

Naomi's Plan

Naomi suspected that Boaz needed some encouragement to step forward and assume the role of kinsman-redeemer. The possibility may not have occurred to him because he was much older than Ruth and because she was a Moabite.

Naomi told Ruth to bathe, put on perfume, and dress in her best clothes. She told her to sneak down to the threshing floor where Boaz was spending the night. Once he had eaten, had plenty of wine, and fallen asleep, Ruth must "uncover his feet" and lie next to him until he noticed her.

Boaz responded exactly as Naomi hoped he would. When he discovered someone at his feet in the darkness, Boaz asked, "Who are you?"

"I am your servant Ruth," she said. "Spread the corner of your garment over me, since you are a kinsman-redeemer." "The LORD bless you, my daughter," he replied. "This kindness is greater than that which you showed earlier: You have not run after the younger men, whether rich or poor. And now, my daughter, don't be afraid. I will do for you all you ask. All my fellow townsmen know that you are a woman of noble character. Although it is true that I am near of kin, there is a kinsman-redeemer nearer than I."

verses 9–12 NIV

Boaz solved the next-of-kin problem, and he and Ruth married. They soon had a son. Life for Naomi was full, and Naomi was again pleasant. Her losses behind her, she now had a daughter, a son-in-law, a grandchild, a new life, and a renewed confidence in God.

You have to wonder why Naomi had not thought of Boaz earlier or the other possible kinsman-redeemer, the one whom Boaz mentioned. Perhaps it was because Ruth was a foreigner, and as much as Naomi loved her, she doubted that the men of Bethlehem would want to marry her. But it could also be because she was depressed.

Many people who are depressed feel as if they are in a fog; visibility is poor. They do not see options. Truly they feel as if there is nothing they can do about their situation. This is why medication is helpful to some depressed people; it clears the mind so they see possibilities on how to handle their dilemmas—the ones that made them depressed in the first place.

People who are ruminators with distorted or pessimistic thoughts prolong their depressions, and the swirling thoughts are hard to stop. Often some kind of distracting action will break up their power. Ruth's report broke up Naomi's pessimistic thinking, giving her a sense of possibility, propelling her forward into the future and out of the pit of depression. What would Naomi have done without Ruth?

The Importance of Friends

When there was no one else, no family members, Ruth was there for Naomi. When Ruth could have graciously bowed out of their relationship, she didn't; instead, she committed herself to Naomi and accompanied her back to Bethlehem, not to stay with her temporarily but to stay with her until death parted them. When Naomi was bitter, Ruth patiently hung on. When they needed a way to provide for themselves, Ruth went to work. And in God's providence, he led Ruth to Boaz's field, which enabled Ruth to come home with good news. This news set in motion the events that would change Naomi's life.

Naomi's friends saw how much she valued Ruth's friendship. After her grandson was born, the Bethlehem women gathered around her as they had when she first returned. This time they said, "Praise the Lord! He has given you a grandson today to take care of you. May the boy become famous in Israel! Your daughter-in-law loves you, and has done more for you than seven sons. And now she has given you a grandson, who will bring new life to you and give you security in your old age" (Ruth 4:14–15).

We could all use a Ruth—or Ruths!—in our lives. Life is an unending series of problems to be faced and dealt with. Problems are inevitable, but victory is not, which is why we need friends.

Martin Luther wrote a great deal about depression, something he battled repeatedly. He offered many helpful suggestions for dealing with this problem. He advised against being alone and said we should seek help from

45

others. He wrote, "Seek out some Christian brother, some wise counselor. Undergird yourself with the fellowship of the church."[3] Dining together, singing, joking, and talking with friends interrupt a person's ruminating. The presence of others would also be a comfort, taking away the feelings of alienation and loneliness that sometimes accompany depression. Their wise counsel could shed light on ways to walk out of the darkness.

God never intended for us to face life alone. He made us social creatures and he called us to live in community with God's people—people with whom to share the spirit and the load.

We all need friends and having them can make all the difference when we slip into a dark valley. They can reach for our hand, take hold, walk with us, and sometimes even help us out of the valley. This doesn't mean all friends are helpful when we are in low places. Sometimes just the opposite is true, as we'll see in the next story.

Replay and Reflect

What encouragement does Naomi's story offer you?

If you suddenly had no means of supporting yourself, what would your reaction be?

What are intangible losses?

When is ruminating helpful? When is it not?

Who in your life is like Ruth to you?

How can you be a Ruth to someone else?

(handwritten margin note: We need Christian friends!)

3

◄| Job |►

When Loss Is Catastrophic

If only my anguish could be weighed.

. . . It would surely outweigh the sand of

the seas.

JOB 6:2–3 NIV

*Y*ou're fired" can be some of the most shocking words a person ever hears. My husband heard those words not once but twice within eighteen months. We were both left reeling from the impact.

Several weeks after the second firing, some Christian friends invited us to a potluck. I assumed they wanted to minister to us, and we welcomed it. We felt lonely and fragile as we tried to cope with our circumstances. Several families were involved, and we enjoyed lively conversation while we ate. For a brief interlude, we forgot our troubles.

After the meal was over, the men and children went outside to play ball. As we sipped coffee, the women began questioning me. How was Bob *really* doing? How are *you* managing? What kind of job prospects does Bob have? Unfortunately, I said, "The future looks bleak." The women immediately diagnosed the cause for Bob's unemployment as a lack of faith on my part.

I was just being realistic. Bob was in a field that was oversaturated—too few jobs for too many applicants. Plus anyone fired twice so closely together would have a hard time finding a job. Bob had already said to me several times, "I would have a hard time hiring myself."

I needed friends to pray with me and encourage me. Instead, they began "preaching" to me about my lack of faith. One woman even said, "I don't care what happens to my children or me, God will be obligated to rescue us because of my faith."

As they picked at me, I felt like vultures were attacking. You can imagine my relief when Bob stuck his head in the door and said, "Time to go."

I was limp and quiet on the drive home. Bob said, "What's wrong?"

I said, "I think I've just had a Job experience."

Our losses weren't anywhere near the catastrophic losses that Job experienced, but I could identify with the way Job's friends treated him. Considering the magnitude of his losses, you would think they would have been compassionate.

Job's Losses

Job was a rich man who lived in the land of Uz. He had ten children and owned seven thousand sheep, three thousand camels, one thousand cows, and five hundred donkeys, plus he had a large number of servants. Then quite suddenly, everything changed:

His donkeys were stolen.

Most of his servants were killed.

Lightning struck his shepherds and sheep and killed them all.

Raiders took away the camels.

A storm killed all of his children.

He lost his health.

Loathsome sores broke out all over his body.

Job was so miserable that he sat by the garbage dump where he took a piece of broken pottery and scraped his sores. Amid the rubbish, rotting carcasses, homeless beggars, burning fires, and howling dogs, he pondered his losses. If his "troubles and griefs were weighed on scales, they would weigh more than the sands of the sea" (Job 6:2–3).

Noticing his misery and remembering how good Job was, his wife said to him, "You are still as faithful as ever, aren't you? Why don't you curse God and die?" (2:9).

Was she a tad resentful about Job's being so good? Maybe she thought he was too conscientious at times. He even offered sacrifices to God on behalf of his children in case they had sinned unintentionally. And where did it get him?

"Job answered, 'You are talking nonsense! When God sends us something good, we welcome it. How can we complain when he sends us trouble?' Even in all this suffering Job said nothing against God" (v. 10). This might have been the end of Job's story, giving us a good example of being faithful to God in times of great suffering, if his friends hadn't come to comfort him.

Job, What Have *You* Done?

Eliphaz from Teman, Bildad from Shuah, and Zophar from Naamah, heard about Job's great suffering, so they went to Uz to comfort him. "While they were still a long way off they saw Job, but did not recognize him" (Job 2:12).

They saw a man with a shaved head, torn clothes, and open sores sitting near the garbage dump. This could not be the richest man in the East! When they realized the man was Job, "they began to weep and wail, tearing their clothes in grief and throwing dust into the air and on their heads" (v. 12b).

Stunned into silence by what they saw, the three friends sat on the ground with Job for seven days and nights without saying a word. Job must have taken their silence to mean they sympathized with him, so he assumed he could be honest with them. "Job broke into a curse, not against God, but against his own existence."[1] He wished he had never been born, that he had died at birth, and that he could now die (see chap. 3).

I wish I could tell you the friends nodded their heads in sympathy and said, "We can understand why you feel this way after all you have been through. But, Job, we're here for you. We're going to help you get through this." Instead, Job's raw honesty shocked them, and he appeared to them as lacking in fortitude. They concluded he must have sinned because everyone knows that God rewards good and punishes evil. Eliphaz challenged Job to think back on what he might have done to cause such horrible things to happen to him.

Job defended himself by insisting he had committed no sins worthy of the punishment he was suffering. Job challenged Eliphaz to prove he had sinned, and he asked God to do the same. This made Bildad angry.

Bildad lashed out at Job and called him a windbag. He said, "God never twists justice; he never fails to do what is right" (8:3), so the fault must lie with Job. Of course, none of the friends or Job knew that Satan had asked permission of God to test Job's faithfulness. They were responding according to their traditional religious beliefs. If you sin, you suffer. If you repent, the suffering stops. Consequently, the visit that was meant to comfort turned into confrontation.

Dueling Dialogue

The friends grilled Job, and he fired back. He defended his record and asked pointed questions. He insisted he had done nothing wrong, certainly nothing to deserve the treatment he had received. Besides, if God only rewarded the righteous, then why did he allow the wicked to defeat them? Why did he let the wicked prosper? They were not righteous and yet they were blessed.

Zophar told Job he was talkative and boastful. He said, "God is punishing you less than you deserve" (Job 11:6). What a low blow to deliver to someone who was already down! And then Zophar insisted that Job repent. He said, "Put your heart right, Job. Reach out to God. Put away evil and wrong from your home" (vv. 13–14).

Job insisted that he didn't need to repent. He insisted that he would continue to trust in the Lord even if God killed him. Still, it would mean so much to him if he just knew what God's complaints against him were, if he could just have an audience with God. His friends told him that he was foolish to even expect such a thing. God would never personally answer his questions.

A bystander, a young man named Elihu, who had heard much of the arguing, was angered by what he heard. To him, Job was justifying himself and blaming God. Job's three friends could not find any way to answer Job sufficiently so "this made it appear that God was in the wrong" (32:3). Elihu took it upon himself to be God's defense lawyer, but he did a poor job. He covered much of the same ground as the other friends had and said little that was new. Like the others, he insisted that Job should repent and that God would not personally answer his questions.

You have to wonder if these people were really Job's friends. They had no compassion for his misery. Instead, they said Job acted as if the whole world should stop just because he was suffering, as if it were no big deal. But it was a big deal, so big that Job was depressed.

Job's Depression

Within the comments Job made to his friends and to Elihu, we see the symptoms of depression. Like Naomi, Job was bitter. And he seemed to have to talk about it, to let it out, more than Naomi did. He said, "I can't be quiet! I am angry and bitter. I have to speak" (Job 7:11).

And like both Naomi and Moses, he was hopeless:

"Why go on living when I have no hope?" (6:11).

"My days pass by without hope" (7:6).

"My days have passed; my plans have failed; my hope is gone" (17:11).

"Where is there any hope for me?" (17:15).

Job felt intense inner turmoil, like the wretchedness that Moses experienced. He said, "I have no peace, no rest, and my troubles never end" (3:26).

And like Moses, he wanted to die to escape the misery he was in. Life just wasn't worth living any longer:

"I am sick of living. Nothing matters" (9:21).

"I am tired of living" (10:1).

"My only hope is the world of the dead" (17:13).

"Month after month I have nothing to live for" (7:3).

Not only did he want to die, his grief over the way his life had turned out was so extensive that he wished he had never been born. Not only did he want God to curse the day he was born, but he wanted him to curse the night he was conceived (3:3). He wished he could blot out his existence so that not even a minuscule particle of him remained.

But Job's symptoms were more numerous than those of Naomi and Moses, and we need to be aware of some of them if we want to be able to recognize depression. Depression comes in many forms and guises, and these will vary from individual to individual, and even episodes experienced by the same person may vary.

Job experienced some of the physical changes that go along with depression. Job's appetite changed and he had trouble sleeping:

"Instead of eating, I mourn" (3:24).

"I have no appetite for food" (6:7).

"I am skin and bones, and people take that as proof of my guilt" (16:8b).

"My grief has almost made me blind; my arms and legs are as thin as shadows" (17:7).

"When I lie down to sleep, the hours drag; I toss all night and long for dawn" (7:4).

His strength was reduced. Fatigue often accompanies depression. Job said that he had no strength left to save himself (6:11, 13).

Tears flowed freely. Job said, "I have cried until my face is red, and my eyes are swollen and circled with shadows" (16:16), and "My friends scorn me; my eyes pour out tears to God" (v. 20).

But his tears and anguish did not go unnoticed by God. He loved Job so much that he appeared to him (38:1). Job had passed Satan's test, and God was ready to minister to him.

Job's "Aha" Moment

At this point in reading Job's story, I'm anticipating that God will give him a reason for his losses. Perhaps he will tell him about Satan's request to test his faith or give him some other satisfying answer. It would just make him feel good; it would make all the pieces of the puzzle fit. But that's not what happened. God didn't give Job an answer. Instead, he asked him questions.

God started with "Where were you when I laid the earth's foundation?" (38:4 NIV) and went on to such questions as "Who waters the dry and thirsty land, so that grass springs up?" (v. 27) and "Do you know when mountain goats are born?" (39:1). Question after question was directed to Job,

54

making it clear to him that God is mighty, wise, and powerful. He is the one who created and controls the sea, the light, the underworld, and the weather. He also understands and controls the lion, deer, ox, ostrich, horse, and bird of prey.

Then suddenly God interrupted his recital and said, "Job, you challenged Almighty God; will you give up now, or will you answer?" (40:2).

Job answered, "I spoke foolishly, Lord. What can I answer? I will not try to say anything else. I have already said more than I should" (40:4–5).

Even though what God said humbled Job and he admitted that he had talked too much, God was not finished. He challenged Job to think about justice. "Are you trying to prove that I am unjust—to put me in the wrong and yourself in the right? Are you as strong as I am?" (40:8–9).

Following this probing, God continued his recital of the wonders of creation and its management. As God spoke, Job began to see that something bigger than he could see was going on. That's when Job had his "aha" moment. There was more to God than he had previously known. He said, "In the past I knew only what others had told me, but now I have seen you with my own eyes" (42:5).

God was different from what he had always thought, and this realization led him to repent in dust and ashes. Knowing "why" lost its importance. Job was still impoverished, bereft of his children, and sick to death, but he no longer believed that God was against him or had abandoned him. His inner turmoil ceased and was replaced by peace.

And then God vindicated Job by chiding his friends because they did not speak the truth about him the way Job had. He told Job to intercede and make offerings for his friends because their accusations had been way off base.

That Job readily prayed for his friends was further evidence of his sterling character. He was indeed a good man who desired to obey God.

After Job prayed, God prospered him with greater blessings than he had known before his losses and subsequent depression. He fathered more children and enjoyed four generations of offspring until he died full of years, offering proof that there is life after depression. We need this reminder, because when we are depressed we tend to think life will never be good again.

Blessed Days Ahead

The Bible says, "The LORD blessed the latter end of Job more than his beginning" (Job 42:12 KJV). How can we get to that place of blessing? While there is no set route, Job's story shows us we may have to relinquish our right to know why, allow our thinking to be challenged, and pray for those who hurt us.

Surrendering Our Right to Know Why

Blessed is the person who knows why he or she is depressed, because not knowing weighs heavily on a person's mind. *Why? Why do I feel this way? What did I do to deserve this? It wouldn't be so hard to bear if I just knew why.*

To keep contemplating the reasons why can bog you down so you can't think about the present or the future. You get stuck in the mud at the bottom of the depression pit, and it holds you there. In the meantime, days or weeks are passing by when you could be getting on with life.

Job never discovered why he was tested. He never knew what we know from reading the book that it was Satan, not God, who had initiated all his suffering—yet he came to be

56

at peace with God and with himself. He learned and grew from the experience and went on to have a rich, full life.

To give up our right to know why doesn't mean we will never know. It just means we are willing to let it go, trust God, and move on with life.

Allowing Our Thinking to Be Challenged

Where do you get your ideas about God and what he is like? Do they come from deep Bible study or someone's earnest preaching? Are they concepts repeated by friends, written about in religious literature, or repeated over and over in Sunday school so often that they have lodged in your mind? Have these concepts ever been challenged? Sometimes they need to be, and depression can be the catalyst for doing just that.

Dr. John White wrote in his book *The Masks of Melancholy: A Christian Physician Looks at Depression and Suicide* about a forty-year-old bachelor who was convinced he was too bad for God to forgive him. The patient had been in the psychiatric ward for several weeks. The man believed he had cancer and that all the medical personnel were lying to him when they told him he showed no evidence of it. "He had no energy and no appetite, and he couldn't sleep. He was given antipsychotic pills, mood-elevating pills, and ten electroconvulsive treatments," but there was no change.

Two things really seemed to bother the man. He had drunk a bottle of beer several years before when his doctor had told him not to. More significantly, he had avoided enlisting in World War II and felt bad that some of his friends had died in Europe.

One day as they talked, White asked, "What about forgiveness?"

The man answered, "I want it so *bad*."

"What's your religion?"

"Russian Orthodox."

"And what does your priest say about how you get to be forgiven?"

"He doesn't talk too much. I go to confession."

"And what does that do?"

"I don't often go."

White groped for words. "But if you do go, why would God forgive you?"

"Because Christ died. He shed blood."

"*So?*"

"But I'm too bad for that."

For no logical reason, White grew angry. "What d'you mean you're too bad?"

The patient raised his voice as White's was getting louder. He said, "I don't deserve ever to be forgiven."

"You're darn right you don't!"

The patient looked up at White surprised. "I can't be a hypocrite. I gotta make amends."

White found his anger increasing. "And who d'you think you are to say Christ's death was not enough for you? Who are you to feel you must add your miserable pittance to the great gift God offers you? Is his sacrifice not good enough for the likes of you?"

Just as God's questions humbled Job, White's questions humbled this man. The patient began both to cry and to pray at once, asking God for forgiveness. As he experienced it, he thanked God over and over.

His eyes were shining as he shook White's hand. "Thanks, Doc. Thanks a lot. How come nobody ever told me before?"

White cut out all the medication. During the following week, he deliberately refrained from doing more than bid the patient, "Good morning, how are you?" each day. He wanted to let others record his progress, and they did. The notes on his chart read, "Remarkable improvement. No longer seems depressed. Paranoid ideation not expressed. Making realistic plans for the future."[2]

Stuck in both Job's mind and the patient's mind were not quite accurate pictures of God. When their thoughts were challenged, they began to see God in a greater, more profound, and life-changing way.

Praying for Others

As we noted in Naomi's story, we need friends to help us through the twists and turns of life. Friends can offer solutions to problems, listen when we want to talk, and provide valuable support. While we can mostly gauge who these people are, sometimes our friends surprise us. They might pull away, as depressed people are sometimes hard to be around. They might think our complaints are petty. They might disagree with us theologically, as Job's friends did with him. They might make cutting remarks as Bildad did when he said to Job, "Your children must have sinned against God, and so he punished them as they deserved" (Job 8:4). Or as Zophar said to Job, "God is punishing you less than you deserve" (11:6).

We might be so hurt by any of these responses that we sulk and replay the scenes over and over. I know, because I did. When I told Bob about the comments the women at the potluck made, he sloughed them off. I might have done the same thing if a letter hadn't come from one of the women two days later. When I saw the return address, I thought, *How nice! An apology.* But when I opened the letter, I found another accusation. The writer said I was refusing to forgive the man who fired Bob. News to me! I was so worried about our future I hadn't even given him a thought.

I was so irked by her unfounded accusation that I started mentally replaying over and over her comments and the ones others made in the weeks ahead. Their comments never caused me to become depressed, but they speeded up the downward spiral that would eventually come. I wish I could say I readily prayed for them as Job did, but I didn't. It took me months when recovery was finally underway for me to pray, "Father, forgive them, for they know not what they do." When I did, God blessed the latter days of Brenda Poinsett more than the beginning, and he can do the same for you.

Replay and Reflect

Do you think Job might have responded differently if he had known that God had permitted Satan to test him?

Was Job a patient man as James 5:11 (KJV) describes him?

Many people have said, "The book of Job is every man's story." Is it? Does everyone have a Job experience sometime in life?

What was the power of questions in Job's story? What did they accomplish?

How can a person surrender his or her right to know why?

Why was it wise to have Job pray for his friends? Would it have anything to do with the wisdom in James 5:16?

"Therefore confess your sins to each other and pray for each other so that you may be healed. The prayer of a righteous man is powerful and effective."

4

⊰| Hannah |⊱

When You're Desperate

I am desperate, and I have been praying
. . . because I'm so miserable.

1 SAMUEL 1:15–16

*R*ecently I read a news article about the rate of rural suicide in Australia.[1] Currently it is among the highest in the world, as farmers battle the stress of years of drought and failed crops. They are devastated not to be able to produce crops and feed their families. One farmer said, "The strain is just so constant and long. It's like someone grabbing me by the throat and slowly choking me a bit more each day." Reacting to this dilemma is not a simple matter of changing jobs and moving to cities.

Being a farmer is in their blood; it is their personal and occupational identity.

I was in a growth group once with a sweet, pretty woman whose husband had shocked her by asking for a divorce. The divorce had been some years earlier but to her it was just as if it had happened yesterday. Even though her days were filled with a job, mothering two teenagers, and church activities, she wasn't happy. I don't know how many times she said to our group, "I never saw myself as being anything but a wife and mother. That is all I ever wanted."

Have you ever wrestled with something like this, something you can't change that also affects your core being? If you have, then you will identify with Hannah, a woman who wanted very much to have children but couldn't. Yet for Hannah, being a woman meant having children.

This kind of situation provides ripe conditions for growing depression because it packs a double punch. You're dealing with something you have no control over plus the loss of who you are. In Hannah's case, her situation was exacerbated by a third factor—the presence of another woman.

One of Two

Hannah was the wife of Elkanah, a man with two wives, an arrangement that seems strange to us. Although God's original intention for marriage was between one man and one woman (Gen. 2:24), some leaders in early biblical times, such as Abraham, Jacob, and David, had more than one wife. Polygamy was not a normal practice for ordinary Israelites, but bigamy seems to have been. Deuteronomy contains a law to regulate the custom (21:15–17), so evidently the arrangement was permissible.

The main reason for men to have more than one wife was to guarantee children. The Israelites feared childlessness.

- Children were a very important part of the economic structure of society. They were a source of labor for the family. The family's income and survival were dependent on children.
- Numerous children were a symbol of status and wealth. God's people believed that a large family was a reward for virtue, a sign of God's blessing.
- Having children ensured the continuation of a man's family line. This is how God's people thought of themselves as living on after death. You survived in your children who would keep your name alive.

With so much riding on having children, you can imagine the pressure put on a married woman. It was "a great indignity for a wife to be unable to bear her husband children."[2] Hannah felt the pressure.

Children were so important that a husband was permitted to divorce a barren wife. Hannah was fortunate that Elkanah remained faithful to her despite the fact that she couldn't conceive. She didn't feel fortunate, though, because Hannah wanted to have children. Her desire wasn't just a response to societal pressure; it was a part of her nature, rooted deep within her. It was what being a woman was all about. In her growing-up years, she saw herself becoming a mother, and now it looked like her dream wasn't going to come true. This made her sad and made her feel like a failure. Feeling this way, she couldn't help but compare herself to Peninnah, the "other woman" in Elkanah's life.

While bigamy was common and acceptable, this didn't mean the arrangement worked well. Marriage triangles were fraught with possibilities for tension, especially between the two wives.

Hannah versus Peninnah

When two women live in the same household and are married to the same man, competition and comparison are naturally going to occur. What the other does is just so "in your face" that you can't help but notice. And if you are the least bit insecure—and who wouldn't be in a marriage triangle where divorce was easily attainable—you question everything. You watch your husband's responses. Is he happy? What makes him notice you? What pleases him? What does he want? Whom does he favor?

In competing for your husband's affection and attention, you become very aware of the other woman's strengths and weaknesses.

Peninnah's major strength was that she was fertile, producing children that would keep her husband's name alive and ensure family income. The Bible makes the contrast between the two women quite clear in one telling line: "Peninnah had children, but Hannah had none" (1 Sam. 1:2 NIV).

Hannah, though, wasn't without assets. She had Elkanah's love. He was devoted to her and favored her. The attention he lavished on Hannah did not escape Peninnah's eyes. Seeing how Elkanah looked at Hannah, perhaps Peninnah sometimes found herself resenting all the work involved in caring for children. Even though she was pleased to be able to have children, still, at times, she was wistful. *Oh, if I just didn't have so much to do. I wish Elkanah looked at me the way he looks at Hannah.*

Although she tried not to, Hannah looked at Peninnah with envy. Peninnah was getting to do what most successful wives did—have children. Even though she cared for Peninnah's children—because they were Elkanah's offspring—she still wanted to carry a child in her womb, give birth, hold a little one, and nurse him at her breast. She felt worthless not being able to do what a woman was designed to do and what wives were supposed to do.

Peninnah sensed how she felt and took advantage of Hannah's vulnerability to prove she was the superior wife. The Bible refers to Peninnah as Hannah's rival or adversary (v. 6). It's interesting that the Hebrew for *rival* or *adversary* "is derived from the root 'to vex' and is used only of a fellow wife."[3] To vex Hannah is what Peninnah set out to do. She tormented and humiliated Hannah, scoffed and laughed at her, because she did not have children. She even implied that her barrenness was a sign of divine displeasure (vv. 6–7).

Peninnah scoffed, taunted, and laughed at Hannah to irritate and provoke her. With accurate precision, she aimed for Hannah's most tender spot and never missed her target. It was her one-upmanship over Hannah. Though Hannah had Elkanah's love, Peninnah had his children. This was painfully obvious to both women when the whole family went to Shiloh to worship.

Family Time at Shiloh

Each year Elkanah and his family—yes, both wives went!—journeyed to the tabernacle at Shiloh, the religious center at that time for Israelites. They went to worship the Lord, which included making an animal sacrifice.

Part of the sacrificial animal was offered to God; the rest was consumed by the worshipers. This meant that Elkanah, his wives, and children had a feast while at Shiloh. Having meat to eat made this a very special occasion, but the festive atmosphere was marred by a jealous wife.

After Elkanah made the sacrifice, he gave "portions of the meat to his wife Peninnah and to all her sons and daughters. But to Hannah he gave a double portion because he loved her, and the LORD had closed her womb" (1 Sam. 1:4–5 NIV). Peninnah noticed this special attention and did a slow burn. She was the dutiful wife, the fertile wife bearing her husband children; she should be the favored one. Obviously she wasn't, so she picked at Hannah and irritated her, reminding her over and over of what she could not have. Finally Hannah could bear it no longer. She didn't retaliate; she didn't fight back. Instead, she became depressed:

Her appetite changed. She couldn't eat.
She was sorrowful.
She was filled with anguish and grief.
She wept over her dilemma.
Her countenance changed.

While depression isn't always recognizable in another person, often it is, especially when you can see symptoms such as appetite change, weeping, and a change in facial expression. Elkanah was a sensitive man. He noticed Hannah's symptoms. He recognized that something was wrong and connected her sadness to her barrenness. He asked her, "Hannah, why are you crying? Why won't you eat? Why are you always so sad? Don't I mean more to you than ten sons?" (v. 8).

Trying to help, Elkanah assured Hannah that the love and consideration she received from him was better than what having ten sons would have done for her. This comment did not make Hannah feel better! While he was trying to help, Elkanah did not grasp the full depth of Hannah's pain. It was about more than being loved; it involved who she was as a person and her purpose in life. He responded in a way an adult might respond to a depressed teenager, "What do you have to be depressed about? You've got your whole life ahead of you." The speaker, voicing what he assumes to be words of comfort, just sees the surface and does not realize the depth of inner pain.

The person who is trying to help the depressed person finds it baffling that words like this do not help. The depressed person wants someone to take the time to really understand the reason for his or her grief. Hannah knew her husband loved her, but it was not enough to heal her aching heart. She had to make contact with someone who could understand and help.

Hannah's Visit to the Tabernacle

Once they finished the communal meal, Hannah went to the tabernacle. In deep anguish she cried bitterly and prayed to the Lord. Hannah prayed at length, honestly expressing her feelings and her true longing. Most of her prayer is not in the Bible, but it does give her vow. She prayed, "O Lord of heaven, if you will look down upon my sorrow and answer my prayer and give me a son, then I will give him back to you, and he'll be yours for his entire lifetime, and his hair shall never be cut" (1 Sam. 1:11 TLB).

Hannah wanted a child so much that if she had a son, she would give him back to God. Her promise that his hair would never be cut probably meant that Hannah was making a Nazirite vow, which set her son apart for special service to God. An individual could make a Nazirite vow, and parents could make one for their unborn children. As long as the vow was in effect, the person's hair could not be cut. Although some Nazirite vows were temporary, Hannah's vow was for life.

To some, Hannah's prayer is beautiful. She was so sincere, so trusting, and so willing to give to God. Her prayer has given hope to thousands. In her name, organizations and websites provide comfort and give support to couples facing infertility, miscarriage, or neonatal loss.

Some people criticize her prayer because she bargained with God, something, they say, mature believers shouldn't do. We should grow in our trust and in our faith in God and be so conscious of his will that we know what to ask and how to ask for it. We don't need to make bargains.

Some say her prayer was a selfish one. She was not thinking of Elkanah. After all, he already had children and didn't need for her to have a baby. Neither was she asking on behalf of God's people or the greater good of mankind. She was only thinking of herself. One commentator said, "There is no moral reason why God, if he could, should respond to her plea."

I've been a student of prayer longer than I've been a student of depression, and I don't fault Hannah for praying the way she did. Hannah was a desperate woman and knew God was her only source. If God had closed her womb, as Elkanah and Peninnah had said he had, then God was the one who could open it. Hannah didn't have many other options. Plus she was a woman of faith. She did not have an "*if* he could" in her mind. It was a matter of "if he *would*." If he did, then she would be so grateful that she would give her baby back to God. Her bargain showed how sincere she was and what a high price she would pay to have the desire of her heart granted. She knew intuitively what the apostle Peter would encourage believers to do many years later. He advised: "Casting all your care upon Him, for He cares for you" (1 Peter 5:7 NKJV).

Hannah's prayer has comforted and reassured me on several occasions. Her honest, fervent prayer and God's answer encourage me to pray about perceived impossibilities in my own life. *God, this is Hannah speaking. I am a desperate woman, and you are the only one who can help. You are my Rock, my Source, my Salvation.*

While her prayer was and is a personal encouragement to me, I'll admit I was uneasy writing about it for this book. In writing about Moses, Naomi, and Job, I could say, Follow their examples when you are depressed and you will find relief. If it is accumulated stress, share the load. If it is ruminating about concerns, break it up by taking action. If you can't figure out why bad things happen, give up the quest and allow your thinking to be expanded. But now with Hannah's example, I can't say, Pray like she did, and he will *for sure* give you the desires of your heart. I can't guarantee how God will respond; I can only assure you that he will. God responds to honest prayer. God will answer *you*.

God Answers Hannah

Eli, the priest, was sitting at his customary place beside the entrance of the tabernacle while Hannah prayed. He "watched her lips. She was praying silently; her lips were moving, but she made no sound" (1 Sam. 1:12–13). He thought this odd, as most people usually prayed aloud. He assumed she was drunk. Apparently drunken excess occurred at the Shiloh feasts, so he associated Hannah's behavior with drinking.

Irritated, Eli said to her, "Stop making a drunken show of yourself! Stop your drinking and sober up!" (v. 14).

"'No, I'm not drunk, sir,' she answered. 'I haven't been drinking! I am desperate, and I have been praying, pouring out my troubles to the Lord. Don't think I am a worthless woman. I have been praying like this because I'm so miserable'" (vv. 15–16).

Either her forthrightness or her determination convinced Eli of her sincerity. He responded by joining her in prayer that God would grant her request and give her his blessing. He said to her, "Cheer up! May the Lord of Israel grant you your petition, whatever it is!" (v. 17 TLB).

The fact that this man of God would add his prayer to hers lifted Hannah's spirit. Her honest prayer and Eli's words transformed Hannah. She said to Eli, "'May your servant find favor in your eyes.' Then she went her way and ate something, and her face was no longer downcast" (v. 18 NIV).

Hannah had been discouraged to the point of being physically sick and unable to eat, but after her honest prayer and Eli's reassuring words, her countenance changed and she could eat. The depression lifted even though she was still not pregnant. This could mean one of two things. She was at peace about her situation, ready to accept what she could not change. Or she knew for certain that God was going to give her a child. Many earnest pray-ers receive this kind of inner reassurance before they ever see the actual answer. Either way, God answered Hannah, and she became pregnant.

A Son Is Born

When they returned home, Elkanah slept with Hannah, and she conceived a child. Nine months later a baby boy was born to her. "She named him Samuel (meaning 'asked of God') because, as she said, 'I asked the Lord for him'" (1 Sam. 1:20 TLB).

The next year Elkanah and Peninnah and her children went on the annual trip to the tabernacle without Hannah, for she told her husband she was not going with him and the others that year. "Wait until the baby is weaned, and then I will take him to the Tabernacle and leave him there."

"'Well, whatever you think best,' Elkanah agreed. 'May the Lord's will be done'" (vv. 22–23 TLB).

So Hannah stayed home and didn't make the trips to Shiloh until Samuel was probably two or three years old. When Samuel was weaned, Hannah fulfilled her vow. She and Elkanah took young Samuel to the tabernacle. They also took along a three-year-old bull for the sacrifice, a bushel of flour, and some wine. When they had slaughtered the bull, they took Samuel to Eli, and Hannah gave back to God what he had given her.

Hannah said to Eli, "Sir, do you remember me? . . . I am the woman who stood here that time praying to the Lord! I asked him to give me this child, and he has given me my request; and now I am giving him to the Lord for as long as he lives" (vv. 26–28 TLB).

Hannah left Samuel with Eli to serve as his assistant, and she and Elkanah returned home. Now that's when I would have become depressed! I would never have been able voluntarily to give up a child at such a young age. I'm sure it wasn't easy for Hannah, but keeping a promise to God was just as much a part of who she was as being a mother. Besides, her heart was full of gratitude; she had gained and grown through the experience.

As a result of honest praying and sincere faith, Hannah was fulfilled as a woman. She was now capable of bearing children; she and Elkanah would have five more. She had enjoyed the time she had with Samuel and would nurture the relationship for years, seeing him regularly at Shiloh and making him linen robes like Eli's. Plus she held within her heart a precious secret; she knew she could take every need to God, and he would respond. This didn't mean he would always give her what she asked for, but it did mean he would answer. He was her Rock and he was a God who balanced out inequalities (see 1 Sam. 2:1–10). The impossible wasn't always impossible, and her innermost needs had been met. No wonder she praised the Lord! This woman who could pray so fervently that she lost all awareness of her surroundings could also fluently verbalize her praise. She sang,

> How I rejoice in the Lord!
> How he has blessed me!
> Now I have an answer for my enemies,
> For the Lord has solved my problem.
> How I rejoice!
> No one is as holy as the Lord!
> There is no other God,
> Nor any Rock like our God.
>
> verses 1–2 TLB

I do not know what makes you feel complete as a person, nor do I know if you are dealing with something that seems unchangeable. I do not know what troubles you. But I do know where you can go for help. Like Hannah, you can go to the God of heaven and earth, who holds all things in his mighty hand. He will hear your honest prayer and he will answer *you*.

Replay and Reflect

What was the hardest thing Hannah had to deal with?

What was the most encouraging thing she had going for her?

How do you feel about Hannah's praying very specifically for a son? Is her example one we should follow?

Have you ever prayed so deeply that you lost awareness of the external world?

When did Hannah's depression lift—after she prayed, after Eli encouraged her, after she conceived, after she gave birth?

What reassurance does Hannah's story offer?

5

ᛣᛁ Saul ᛁᛊ

When Jealousy Rages

I'll pin him to the wall.

1 SAMUEL 18:11

As you listen to Mike Wallace deftly interview someone on *60 Minutes*, would you be surprised to learn that Wallace has suffered from depression? As you watch the talented and attractive Sheila Walsh on stage at a Women of Faith conference, would you believe that she has struggled with depression? What about Buzz Aldrin? Would you be shocked to know that someone who has had the exhilarating experience of going to the moon has also known some terrible down times? As you see Tipper Gore, confident and sparkly, smiling at the television cameras, would you believe it if someone told you she has been depressed?

Because these people are attractive, personable, capable, intelligent, and successful, it is hard to believe that depression has been a part of their lives. You wonder, How could someone like that be depressed?

When we appraise another person, we don't see what's going on inside. While he may appear self-assured and confident, inside he may feel very uncertain about himself. While she may appear calm, she may be a bundle of nerves inside. There's always the unseen operating in a person's life, and the unseen may have been Saul's undoing.

What We Can't See

The tribes of Israel who had been loosely organized during the time of Naomi and Hannah wanted a king. Hannah's boy, Samuel, was a mature man by now, and he served God as a prophet, priest, and judge to the Israelites, so it was up to him to help them make the transition. God told Samuel to be looking for someone from the tribe of Benjamin; he would be the new king. When he saw Saul, a Benjamite who was taller than most fellows, God spoke again to Samuel: "This is the man. Anoint him to be king" (see 1 Sam. 9:17).

Saul had "executive presence" so that when Samuel introduced him as king, the Israelites assumed he had all the attributes needed to be their leader. They shouted, "Long live the king!" (10:24 NIV). The few who had reservations were quickly won over by his courage and ingenuity. So Saul was highly regarded by God, Samuel, and the people. Yet some of Saul's responses show he didn't share their view.

Who, Me?

Saul and a servant were looking for some lost donkeys when Samuel spotted him. Samuel indicated that their meeting was very significant. Saul responded, "I belong to the tribe of Benjamin, the smallest tribe in Israel, and my family is the least important one in the tribe. Why, then, do you talk like this to me?" (1 Sam. 9:21).

You Won't Hear It from Me

The next day, as Saul and his servant were leaving for home, Samuel told Saul that he would receive three signs from God as proof he was God's choice to rule God's people. In succession, he would encounter two men by Rachel's tomb, three men going up to Bethel, and a group of prophets leaving the hill of God in Gibeah. Samuel said, "When you meet the band of prophets, at that moment the Spirit of God will come upon you." All of this happened just as Samuel said, and Saul joined the prophets in their ecstatic dancing and shouting (see 1 Sam. 10:1–10).

This was some pretty amazing verification that God had selected him, yet when Saul's uncle questioned him about his trip, Saul talked about the donkeys but didn't say a word about what had happened or about his being chosen as king (v. 16).

I'd Rather Hide

When Samuel called all the Israelites together to an-nounce Saul's appointment publicly, Saul could not be found. Eventually they discovered him "hiding behind the supplies" (1 Sam. 10:22).

Just because God and others saw potential in Saul didn't mean he was convinced he could unite the twelve tribes or fight their enemies. His inside view of himself didn't match the outside view, so he wasn't quick to assume his new role. He did nothing at first and one day he heard a strange sound. The people of Gibeah were crying.

"What is the matter? Why is everyone weeping?" he asked.

"There were messengers here," a man answered, "sent by our brothers who live in Jabesh. The Ammonite king has attacked them. His army was so strong they saw it was useless to fight, so they offered to surrender and become his slaves. But the king of Ammon has mocked them. He said, 'I will let you live only if I first put out the right eye of every one of you!' He has given them seven days to look for help. That is why we are crying."

When Saul heard these words, the Spirit of God came on him. God empowered him as he had empowered the judges before him. Filled with holy anger, Saul took his oxen, and he cut them into pieces. He called messengers and sent the pieces through all the land of Israel.

"Whoever," Saul said, "does not come to fight with Saul and with Samuel for our brothers in Jabesh, his oxen shall be cut to pieces just as these oxen were!" From all directions Israelites came, joined the battle, and successfully defeated the Ammonites (see 1 Samuel 11).

With this victory, Saul firmly established himself as Israel's leader. Even those few people who hadn't shouted "Long live the king!" were now convinced Saul was the man for the job. Success and admiration can boost a person's self-confidence or add to a person's insecurity if the person doesn't believe he or she is right for the role. Perhaps that's why Saul panicked when leading the fight against the Philistines, Israel's toughest enemy.

Plagued by Insecurity

Saul selected an army of three thousand men to fight the Philistines. Of the three thousand, a thousand fought under Jonathan, Saul's son. Jonathan and his men attacked the fierce, cruel Philistines and were successful. His victory rallied the troops and spurred them on, but when they arrived at Gilgal, the Philistines were already there. Their army was much bigger. They had three thousand chariots, six thousand men on horseback, and so many infantrymen you could hardly count them.

The Israelites were so frightened they hid in the caves and in holes in the ground. Saul, seeing the condition of his troops, wanted to get on with the fighting, but Samuel, who served as God's spokesperson to Saul, had told him earlier to wait for him before starting. He would offer sacrifices to God and tell Saul what God wanted him to do.

Every day Saul's army grew smaller, as terrified men deserted. While his army kept shrinking, he waited. He waited for seven days, the number of days Samuel had said he must wait, and still Samuel did not come.

Seeing his troops scattering, Saul decided not to delay fighting any longer. He was afraid he would have no army left. Taking the prepared animals, he offered the sacrifices.

Then Samuel appeared, and he wasn't pleased. He told Saul, "Your rule will not continue. Because you have disobeyed him, the Lord will find the kind of man he wants and make him ruler of his people" (1 Sam. 13:14).

Although he was king, Saul was to remain subordinate to the Lord whose will was made known through his prophet Samuel. When Saul ignored Samuel's instructions, he was ignoring God. In essence, he was saying, I don't trust your choice or your direction.

Later Samuel came again to Saul with some specific instructions. Samuel said, "God commands you to destroy the Amalekites, one of our old enemies. Destroy every one of them, even their sheep, cattle, and camels" (see 15:3). Saul mustered his forces and did as God commanded. He destroyed the Amalekites, *but* he kept alive the best of their cattle and captured the Amalekite king.

Samuel met Saul as he returned from battle. Saul said, "I have carried out the LORD's instructions."

"What then is this bleating of sheep in my ears? What is this lowing of cattle that I hear?" Samuel asked.

Saul excused his disobedience by saying, "The people spared the best of the animals to sacrifice them to God" (see vv. 13–15).

"To obey is better than sacrifice," Samuel answered. "Because you have rejected the word of the LORD, he has rejected you as king" (see vv. 22–23 NIV).

After Saul had tried unsuccessfully to defend himself, he admitted, "I was afraid of the people and so I gave in to them" (v. 24 NIV). His insecurity still plagued him, and now added to that was guilt, remorse, and disappointment, making him ripe for experiencing depression.

A Distressing Spirit

Even though Saul was technically still king, Samuel turned his attention away from him and toward the person who would be the next king. He anointed David for the position, and "the Spirit of Jehovah came upon [David] and gave him great power" (1 Sam. 16:13 TLB).

Simultaneously, even though Saul was miles away, God "sent a tormenting spirit that filled him with depression and fear" (v. 14 TLB). When the evil spirit tormented Saul, his servants could see the black mood descend. They could tell that something was wrong, and they wanted to help. They said to Saul, "We know that something is bothering you. So say the word, and we will look for someone who knows how to play the harp. Then when the terrible mood comes on you, the man can play his harp, and you will be all right again" (see vv. 15–16).

Saul agreed. He said, "Find someone who plays well and bring him to me" (v. 17 NIV).

The harpist they found was David. His music soothed Saul. From then on, whenever the black mood descended, David got his harp and played for Saul. The distressing spirit would leave him, and he would feel refreshed.

You may be bothered by the Bible's saying that God sent the tormenting spirit. Did God cause Saul's depression? The reason the writer of 1 Samuel said God sent the tormenting spirit is because the Israelites didn't have a formalized theology of evil as we who have the New Testament do. At this juncture in the history of God's people, everything—good and evil—was attributed to the Lord. In time they came to understand that an adversary, distinct from God, affected people adversely.

Nevertheless some people who are depressed may feel that God causes depression. If you don't know why you feel the way you do, in your misery you may wonder, *God, why are you doing this to me?*

But even though you may feel God is to blame, he may not be, any more than he was to blame for Saul's depression. Saul was disobedient to God's instructions given to him through the prophet Samuel. When we are disobedient, we suffer the consequences, which for Saul meant that his descendants would not inherit the throne, he was rejected as king, someone else would take his place, he could no longer count on Samuel's support and advice, and he could no longer rely on God's empowering him. Those were huge losses for Saul, and as we know from the stories of Naomi and Job, loss triggers depression.

Since Saul's condition could be relieved with music, he probably had mild depression. That might have been all there was to it if the musician the servants hired hadn't also been a fearless fighter, compounding Saul's inner problems with insecurity.

The Song That Changed Everything

The Philistines had Goliath the giant on their side. He intimidated everyone but young David. David slew the giant and everyone was amazed. As he, King Saul, and other soldiers were returning from fighting the Philistines, women from every town in Israel came out to meet them. They sang joyful songs, danced, and played tambourines and lyres. "The women sang, 'Saul has killed thousands, but David tens of thousands.' Saul did not like this, and he became very angry. He said, 'For David they claim tens of thousands, but only thousands for me. They will be making him king next!' And so he was jealous and suspicious of David from that day on" (1 Sam. 18:7–9).

When you add anger, jealousy, and suspicion to the sorrow, guilt, fear, and insecurity that Saul was already experiencing, the result was a volatile mix that from time to time erupted in irrational behavior.

- Saul behaved like a madman. On one occasion, "David was playing the harp, as he did every day, and Saul was holding a spear. 'I'll pin him to the wall,' Saul said to himself, and he threw the spear at him twice; but David dodged each time" (vv. 10–11).

- He sent David into battle hoping he would be killed, but David wasn't killed. He "was successful in all he did, because the Lord was with him. Saul noticed David's success and became even more afraid of him" (vv. 14–15).

- He tried to have David killed in his own quarters where he was living with his wife, a daughter of Saul. His wife helped David escape (see 19:11–12).

- He sent his men several times to arrest David when he was with a group of prophets led by Samuel. Each time his men ended up prophesying along with the group and lost their motivation to arrest David, so Saul went after him. He too caught the spirit and danced and shouted like the others, but unlike them he lay naked all day and all night (v. 24).

- Saul threw his spear at his beloved son Jonathan because Jonathan questioned his father's reason for being "determined to kill David" (20:33).

- Saul ordered that eighty-five priests in the village of Nob be executed when he learned that they had given shelter to David. He also had all the other village inhabitants, including children, killed.

These episodes of irrational behavior were not constant. They did not happen every day. There were normal times in between. Consequently many Bible students and scholars have concluded that Saul suffered from manic-depressive disorder or bipolar depression. People with bipolar depression have mood cycles—terrible lows (depression) and inappropriate highs (mania) that can last from several days to months. In between the highs and lows, they feel completely normal.

Feeling unusually irritable is a primary characteristic of mania, and Saul certainly was easily irritated! In a mania phase, a person also acts impulsively and uses poor judgment, which was also true of Saul as evidenced in his throwing spears at people who loved him, dancing nude, and killing all the inhabitants of Nob. A person in a mania cycle doesn't recognize barriers and fails to think through the consequences of his behavior. That was Saul!

On the other hand, Saul could have had repeated episodes of unipolar depression and still have behaved the way he did. If the underlying causes of a person's depression are never fully resolved, he or she can pull out of a depression enough for the physical symptoms to leave, and then something happens that plunges the person back into despair. In severe cases, the person is irrational, having a total break from reality (sometimes called a psychotic break).

Whether Saul's depression was bipolar or unipolar, he never recovered, making his story different from the others we've studied. In the other stories, we are encouraged by the recovery of the people and learn from them what we can do to get well. We don't have that kind of example in Saul. He was an insecure man who took extreme measures to maintain his role. His measures didn't work and finally, hopeless and weak, he took his own life by deliberately falling on his sword when losing a battle. Other than using music to soothe a distressing spirit, Saul's example does not provide us with any positive ways to move out of the valley of despair; still, we can learn from his story.

What We Can Learn

If you look closely at Saul's irrational acts, you will see that they were related to David. In Saul's mind, his misery was all David's fault. If it weren't for him, Saul figured his life would have been okay. He would have succeeded as king and been happy.

My husband and I had a pastor like that once who blamed his troubles on others. We didn't realize this at first when we became a part of the mission congregation he was starting. We were struck right away by Pastor Ted's (not his real name) similarity to Saul. He was not a head taller than everyone else, but he had natural ability and was very likeable. Pastor Ted could play the piano by ear and had a mellow singing voice. He was an interesting and dynamic speaker, and speaking seemed to be so easy for him. Bob and I, two experienced speakers who have to work hard at the craft, marveled at how Pastor Ted could see something or have a conversation with someone during the week and develop a whole sermon around it for Sunday. He was personable, with a direct gaze and a hearty handshake. He had great ideas, and our hearts would quicken as we listened to his dreams for our little church.

Plus Pastor Ted was experienced, something you don't always get in a pastor of a small mission congregation. With Ted as our leader, I was certain the mission would not fail, but then I began to notice the negative comments Ted made about churches and how Christians hurt each other. He had been hurt by several churches in the past, which is why we had an experienced pastor serving our mission congregation.

I also noticed how the ideas he inspired us with never materialized into concrete plans. It was like he was stuck in a holding pattern and couldn't move forward. From time to time I wondered if he could be depressed, but when I saw his smile or heard him sing, I shook my head, "Nah, he couldn't be." But it turns out he was.

Our mission church failed; we closed our doors after ten months. Shortly before Ted left our community, he complained to me of the toll ministry takes on a person.

As if to emphasize how awful it was, he said, "I'm on anti-depressants and have been for months."

My first thought was, *Well, why didn't you tell us?* I realize pastors have to be selective about what they share, but the members of this congregation were faithful, loving, understanding people who had high regard for Ted. Most had known hard times themselves and would have responded with sympathy, prayerful support, and possibly wisdom.

Or why didn't he at least tell me? He knew I was the author of two books on depression, wrote articles about it, and had personally struggled with it. Why didn't he say, "Brenda, am I missing something here? I'm depressed and I don't know why. Do you see anything I can do or should do?"

I'm not a counselor, so I'm not suggesting that I could have led Ted to recovery, but if he had said, "I'm depressed; I need help," he would have been on his way to owning his problem. As one psychologist said, "If you can own the mess you're in, there is hope for you and help available. As long as you blame others, you will be a victim for the rest of your life."

Hope and Help

Taking responsibility requires courage, but it is worth it because taking responsibility ignites resolve, engages the help of others, and improves your vision.

Resolve is important because the road to recovery is full of bumps. You have to really want to get well. Even people who seek professional help, which is recommended for those with serious depression such as bipolar or repeated episodes of unipolar depression, need to take responsibility if they want to get well. They have to resolve to take their medicine, keep their appointments, go to therapy, and cooperate with treatment.

King Saul probably wouldn't have responded well to therapy because he had trouble listening, receiving advice, and answering questions. He ignored Samuel's instructions, which was the same as ignoring God. Both Jonathan and David questioned his actions and tried to reason with him.

In response to Jonathan's and David's questions, Saul wept and swore he would change, but he didn't. Sometimes when our focus is so intent on blaming, we don't really *hear* the questions that our friends, loved ones, or therapist may be asking. Instead, we think, *They don't understand*, and we shrug off their comments and questions. We hold on to our view of things.

But if we admit to others we are depressed, we engage their help. This doesn't mean we have to tell everyone we know, but we can and should tell people who care about us and who can offer support. They can be there for us during those rough spots in the road; they can pray for us and give practical and emotional assistance.

Taking responsibility shifts our focus, and we will see things we never noticed when we were in the haze of depression. As a result, our hope level will rise.

Refusing to take responsibility keeps our focus on the negative. When Ted talked about the troubles in his past churches, I wondered why he couldn't see and appreciate his present church. Our members were some of the most faithful I've ever seen. They drove miles to be there every Sunday and every Wednesday evening. Within the congregation we had three ordained people besides the pastor. My husband and I were both seminary graduates and experienced church leaders. We were part of the mission because we wanted to be involved church members. We could have set the world on fire! Well, at least, our little town! But Ted couldn't see how blessed he was because his focus was on past hurts, just as Saul's focus was on David.

Saul was jealous of David, as if David were robbing him of his reputation of being a great man. The military victories Saul had achieved were never totally his, but he recognized neither his own son's contributions nor the asset David was to him. David was a strong, successful military leader and a loyal follower, and his music soothed Saul.

Saul also had little self-appreciation. Saul's reign was the first step in a long and involved process to develop a united kingdom, which took decades to complete. But Saul failed to see the bigger picture. God was building a kingdom and Saul had launched it, but he never recognized his contribution because he compared himself with David, instead of seeing himself as God saw him. When it comes to depression, what goes on inside is as important as what happens on the outside.

Replay and Reflect

If Saul had fully accepted who he was, what difference would it have made in his response to God's tapping him to be king? What difference would it have made in his leadership?

If Saul could have seen himself the way God saw him, what difference would it have made in his life?

How does our view of ourselves affect our happiness potential?

How can disobeying God be a cause for depression?

What connection do strong negative emotions have with depression?

Why is admitting you have a problem a key to recovery?

88

6

⊰| Elijah |⊱

When You Serve Alone

I have been very zealous for the LORD
God Almighty. . . . I am the only one
left.

1 KINGS 19:10 NIV

*H*ave you ever listened to someone describe a great
spiritual experience and think, *Boy, if something like
that happened to me, I would never doubt God?* Or have you
felt goose bumps pop out on your arms as you hear someone
talk about an unusual supernatural encounter? Did you find
yourself feeling a little wistful? Did you think, *If I ever once
experienced something like that, I would always be pumped*

about serving the Lord? That's how I used to react to Elijah's triumph over the prophets of Baal. Then I grew up!

Over the years I've learned that great spiritual experiences and supernatural encounters may not be enough to sustain faith; they may even contribute to discouragement, which is what happened to Elijah. A dramatic duel where God was the undisputed victor wasn't enough to keep him from becoming depressed. In fact it may have contributed to his depression.

Showdown at Mount Carmel

Elijah was one of many prophets who served as the voice of God to the kings and to God's people. Samuel was the prophet to King Saul. Each prophet had his own particular style and manner of delivery. Elijah was a strong, rugged individualist and a miracle worker. He was deeply concerned about the direction the northern kingdom of Israel was taking under the leadership of King Ahab and his wife Jezebel.

Jezebel was a foreigner and when she came to Jezreel, Israel's capital, to live, she brought her devotion to Baal along. She did everything in her power to promote her religion, including supporting 450 prophets of Baal and 400 prophets of the goddess Asherah. Consequently many Israelites began worshiping Baal and Asherah, getting farther and farther away from God and the expectations he had for his people.

At Jezebel's direction, God's prophets were pursued and eliminated as if they were doing something illegal. Sometimes Elijah hid, and at other times he would courageously make his presence—and God's will—known to the king. Elijah wanted to wake the people up and get them back on course. He urged them to do what God wanted, and he was very forthright about it.

Once he marched into the king's palace and announced that a three-year drought was going to occur. The people weren't concerned. They believed Baal would deliver them, but he didn't. Day after day, week after week, and month after month, no rain came! The grass dried up, crops failed, and dust clogged nostrils. Naturally Elijah, the messenger who predicted the drought, was blamed.

King Ahab said to Elijah, "You are a troublemaker!"

Never missing an opportunity to be blunt, Elijah came right back with, "No, you are the troublemaker." He continued, "You are disobeying the Lord's commands and worshiping the idols of Baal. If this drought hasn't convinced you that Baal is a false god, then order all the people of Israel to meet me at Mount Carmel. Bring along the 450 prophets of Baal and the 400 prophets of Asherah who are supported by Queen Jezebel" (see 1 Kings 18:16–19).

The Israelites came in droves to watch as Elijah set the stage for a showdown between Baal and God. He said to them, "If the LORD [shows he] is God, follow him; but if Baal is God, follow him" (v. 21 NIV).

Each side brought a bull to offer as a sacrifice on the altar prepared on Mount Carmel. Neither side would light the fire; Baal or God would do that. Elijah said, "Let the prophets of Baal pray to their god, and I will pray to the Lord, and the one who answers by sending fire—he is God" (v. 24).

The Baal prophets prayed long, hard, and loudly, even cutting themselves with knives and daggers to try to persuade Baal to answer, but he didn't. They ranted and raved for most of the day to no avail.

When it was Elijah's turn, he had water poured on the altar, making it harder for a fire to start. He approached the altar and confidently prayed, "O Lord, the God of Abraham, Isaac, and Jacob, prove now that you are the God of Israel. . . . Answer me, Lord, answer me, so that this people will know that you, the Lord, are God and that you are bringing them back to yourself" (vv. 36–37).

Whoosh! God sent fire down, and it burned up the sacrifice, scorching the earth and drying up the water. "When the people saw this, they threw themselves on the ground and exclaimed, 'The Lord is God; the Lord alone is God!'" (v. 39).

What a daring act of faith! What concrete results! After a visual spiritual victory like this, it seems that the hero could ride off into the sunset and live happily ever after. The victory sustained Elijah for a while, and with the momentum of that experience, he did some very unusual things.

Super Elijah

The people exclaimed, "'Jehovah is God! Jehovah is God!' Then Elijah told them to grab the prophets of Baal. . . . So they seized them all, and Elijah took them to Kishon Brook and killed them there" (1 Kings 18:40 TLB). In one fell swoop, the Baal prophets were gone!

Next, Elijah predicted to King Ahab that a mighty rainstorm was coming—the drought was going to end! Delighted by the news, Ahab prepared a feast. It was time to celebrate. He was going to enjoy himself. But Elijah could see the rain coming far off in the distance when others couldn't. He knew it was going to be heavy. He said to his servant, "Hurry to Ahab and tell him to get into his chariot and get down the mountain, or he'll be stopped by the rain!" (v. 44 TLB).

Sure enough, clouds soon blackened the sky. A heavy wind brought a terrific rainstorm. In haste Ahab drove his chariot toward Jezreel. Elijah, wild with ecstasy after the victory over Baal, ran in front of the king's chariot. For fifteen miles he ran faster than the horses!

When Ahab arrived in Jezreel, he didn't shake Elijah's hand in gratitude or bow to God acknowledging his reality. He rushed inside the palace to tell Queen Jezebel what had happened. When she learned that her prophets had been killed, she was furious! "She sent a message to Elijah: 'May the gods strike me dead if by this time tomorrow I don't do the same thing to you that you did to the prophets'" (19:2).

Whoa! This was totally unexpected. The duel on Mount Carmel was meant to bring revival, turn the tide, change Jezebel, make her acknowledge the one true God, but it didn't. On top of his keen disappointment, Elijah now feared for his life. Forced by her threat, he sought refuge beyond Jezebel's domain. He went to the southern kingdom of Judah, which was not under Ahab's jurisdiction.

When Elijah and his servant arrived safely in Beersheba, Elijah breathed a sigh of relief. He had managed to escape from Jezebel; he was safe. He would lie low for a while, give it some time, as he had on other occasions. He thought this would be the same as other times when he had been in hiding, but it wasn't.

Images of the last few days flashed through Elijah's mind, and he felt uneasy and confused. He questioned God's leadership, and sadness engulfed him. He couldn't figure out what was happening, so he left his servant behind and headed to the wilderness where he could be alone and think.

Broom Bush Brooding

After walking a whole day in the heat of the wilderness, Elijah sat down under a broom bush, a common desert plant that sometimes grew to a height of ten feet. The bush offered Elijah a little shade against the hot desert sun and provided a spot for contemplation. What good had the confrontation with the prophets of Baal done? A revival among God's people was supposed to have occurred, but it hadn't. They acknowledged he was God but there was no change in their commitment. Jezebel was supposed to have realized that the God of Israel was the real God. What good was all the effort he had put into prophesying? Had anything changed? And what a predicament he was in now! After all he had done for God and the nation, he was having to run for his life! It just wasn't fair.

Elijah was so miserable he wanted to die, and he let God know that. "'I've had enough,' he told the Lord. 'Take away my life. I've got to die sometime, and it might as well be now'" (1 Kings 19:4 TLB).

Elijah had been living a purposeful, meaningful life with lots of drama, action, and excitement, and now within a day or two he wanted to die. How could a person's emotions plummet so fast? How could a person's interest in life change so quickly?

Elijah may have experienced a type of depression that Dr. Archibald Hart wrote about in his book *Coping with Depression in the Ministry and Other Helping Professions.* Hart called it "post-adrenaline blues." After a period of time when a person has pulled out all the stops—when his or her senses were heightened and hopes were high, and when he or she operated at peak physical performance and maybe beyond—a letdown occurs.

- For months a bride plans for her wedding, making sure the event is perfect and spectacular. But when the dress has been packed away and the thank-you notes sent, she feels disillusioned, disappointed, and extremely tired. She just doesn't feel like doing anything and she wonders if the event was worth the effort.

- A politician spends weeks before the election using every available minute to publicize his candidacy. He keeps putting his family and friends on hold and neglecting to take his suit to the cleaners or have the oil changed in his car. He keeps saying to himself, *When the election is over, I will* . . . but when it is over, he doesn't want to be with people at all or be bothered with the mundane chores of life. He just wants to crawl into a hole and hide.

- A minister spends all week focusing on the next Sunday morning. He works on a sermon, designs the service, confers with others, visits prospects, and hopes they will join the church. Every week it is the same, and every Sunday night he is in a foul mood and hides behind the newspaper. He is so irritable that his children avoid him and so does his wife. He is baffled by his negative feelings and wonders, *Am I not a man of faith? What is wrong with me?*

According to Hart, experiencing a letdown, as these people did following a time of intensity, is a physiological reaction. "After any high level of activity, the endocrine system, which is designed primarily to deal with emergencies and threats, produces depression so as to demand time for recuperation."[1] The body is saying, "Whoa, I can only take so much. I need time to recover."

Naturally, since it is a physiological reaction, you feel tired and lethargic, but what's interesting about post-adrenaline blues is that thoughts and emotions are also affected. You may feel sad, angry, or hopeless. Bleak thoughts filled with exaggerations and distortions fill your mind; you're confused and you question things. This may explain what happened to Elijah. When his emotions plummeted and his interest in living changed, he was experiencing post-adrenaline blues. Elijah was super, but he wasn't superhuman. When the high drama ceased and his energy was depleted, he was depressed. That's when he prayed, "I've had enough, Lord. Take my life."

God's Answer

In response to Elijah's honest prayer, God didn't take his life. Instead he renewed it, by mercifully and patiently working with him.

Elijah's Physical Needs

God began with Elijah's physical needs. After he prayed, Elijah fell into a deep sleep. God's angel touched him and told him to get up and eat. Eat? Eat what? Elijah looked around and saw some bread baking on hot stones and a jar of water. Just what he needed! He ate the bread, drank the water, and went back to sleep.

"Then the angel of the Lord came again and touched him and said, 'Get up and eat some more, for there is a long journey ahead of you'" (1 Kings 19:7 TLB). His physical recovery would involve more than sleep, food, and drink. It would also involve exercise and solitude.

Elijah got up, ate, drank, and then walked forty days and forty nights to Mount Horeb, the holy mountain of God. The long walk over barren, isolated land allowed him to experience the benefits of solitude and exercise. Many of us live such busy lives that we never discover that solitude brings healing to a weary body and soul. As a tool for battling depression, solitude is not what Martin Luther suggested. Luther said a depressed person should avoid being alone. Being with others keeps a person from ruminating and takes away the loneliness that often accompanies depression. But when, like Elijah, you are physically, spiritually, and emotionally exhausted, solitude is needed. Solitude refreshes and protects a person from having to deal with more stress while trying to recuperate. People recovering from post-adrenaline blues may find even mild stress intolerable.

Exercise can also make a dramatic difference in how you feel. It builds up a person's physical strength, relieves pent-up tension, and works as a mood elevator or antidepressant.

Elijah may not have experienced the full benefits of walking because he was in a bleak mood by the time he arrived at Mount Horeb. While he was physically improving, his mind was still working. Alone while he walked, he could ruminate. So God was going to need to help him with his thinking.

Elijah's Need to Talk

At Mount Horeb Elijah went into a cave to spend the night. The darkness of the cave matched the darkness of his mood. He was physically better, but he was still disappointed about the way things had turned out. He felt sorry for himself. Why go on? Why try so hard when it didn't seem to make any difference? Others didn't care about doing what was right. Was he the only one really serving the Lord?

Elijah was free from Ahab and Jezebel, but he was a prisoner of his own thoughts and emotions, so God invited Elijah to talk. He asked him a very simple question: "Elijah, what are you doing here?" He wasn't looking for an explanation of his geographical location as in, "What are you doing at Mount Horeb?" God was giving Elijah a chance to vent his emotions and talk about what was bothering him.

Elijah's answer revealed what he was thinking and feeling. He said, "Lord God Almighty, I have always served you—you alone. But the people of Israel have broken their covenant with you, torn down your altars, and killed all your prophets. I am the only one left—and they are trying to kill me!" (1 Kings 19:10).

God asked Elijah the same question a second time, "Elijah, what are you doing here?" Not surprisingly, Elijah gave the same answer. I say "not surprisingly" because if you are depressed you go over and over what is bothering you. Saying once what's bothering you doesn't automatically turn off the ruminating, but it does reduce the intensity and releases some emotion. Asking again freed up inner space for God to reorient Elijah's thinking.

God's Challenge

From Elijah's answer to God's question, you can see his thinking isn't quite accurate. Not *all* the Israelites had broken the covenant, not *every* altar had been torn down, and not *all* of God's prophets were killed. In fact

Elijah himself had a conversation with Obadiah, a devout believer, before he asked King Ahab to join him at Mount Carmel. But as he nursed his wounds and felt sorry for himself, he concluded that he was the only faithful one left.

God reminded Elijah that he wasn't alone; there were seven thousand other people alive in Israel who were loyal to God and had not bowed to Baal or kissed his idol. Elijah was not the only faithful one left!

God was also going to correct Elijah's theology. He said, "Go out and stand on the mountain in the presence of the LORD, for the LORD is about to pass by" (1 Kings 19:11 NIV).

God sent a furious wind that split the hills and shattered the rocks, but the Lord wasn't in the wind. After the wind stopped blowing, there was an earthquake, but the Lord was not in the earthquake. After that there came a fire, but God was not in the fire. Where was God? If he was going to pass by, where was he? That's when Elijah heard it—a still small voice, a whisper. And that's when Elijah had an "aha" moment. He realized that believing in God is not a matter of fireworks and spectacular displays, as awe-inspiring as they might be. Believing is a matter of the heart. Is the heart devoted? Does the person love God and want to follow him?

This meant if he went back to being a prophet, he was going to have to help the people develop an intimate relationship with God—so that they could also hear the still small voice. He would have to be patient with people as he worked to instill devotion and fellowship among them. But could he go back? After leaving the way he had, after succumbing to despair, after not getting it right, would God still use him?

God's Direction

God got Elijah moving. God said to Elijah, "Return to the wilderness near Damascus and enter the city" (see 1 Kings 19:15). Movement is very important to counteract the lethargy that accompanies depression. Lethargy can get a grip on you and hold you down until you feel as if you can't move. Some physical action, some duty to perform can propel you forward, getting you unstuck, but it can be very hard to motivate yourself to take this kind of action. So God reached out his hand to Elijah. In giving him direction, it was as if God were saying, "Let me lead you, let me pull you out of the cave and off the mountain now that you are feeling better and thinking more clearly."

But God didn't just give Elijah any old action to get him moving. God gave Elijah meaningful work to do, restoring his confidence as one of God's spokespersons. God was salvaging his life and ministry. He said to Elijah, "Anoint Hazael as king of Syria; anoint Jehu son of Nimshi as king of Israel, and anoint Elisha son of Shaphat from Abel Meholah to succeed you as prophet" (vv. 15–16).

Following the Lord's instructions—taking hold of his hand—Elijah left behind the mountain and his despair. He found Elisha plowing with a team of oxen; there were eleven teams ahead of him. Elijah linked up with them. He took off his cloak and put it on Elisha and as he did so, he knew in a profound way that he was not the only faithful one in Israel. The prophet who had been wrapped up in himself, cooped up in a cave of self-pity, was now happily back at work. This man who once wanted to end his life was now able to face Queen Jezebel, deal with the conflict of religions, and handle the challenges of his own life.

I find that encouraging, and I hope you do too. This life of ours is like a roller coaster not an escalator. We have times of peak spiritual experiences, but we also have dips. I've learned that supernatural encounters and goose-bump-raising experiences, as awesome as they might be, do not prevent dips from occurring. This doesn't mean I don't enjoy hearing about them. I still delight in the retelling of the duel on Mount Carmel by a dramatic, dynamic preacher. I listen with joy, but I listen wisely. I know the spectacular will not guarantee faith, ensure steady commitment, or prevent depression. Something more is needed—a gentle voice that persistently says, "You are precious to me, and I have meaningful work for you to do. Take my hand and walk with me."

Replay and Reflect

Has God ever asked you, What are you doing here?

Can a person become spiritually exhausted?

Was the place where Elijah was hiding significant to his recovery?

In the wind, earthquake, and fire, God displayed his power to Elijah. Was this display important to Elijah's recovery?

What is there about depression that could cause Elijah not to realize there were seven thousand other people faithful to God?

What do God's responses to Elijah's depression teach us about how to respond to depression? What do they teach us about responding to the depression of others?

7

☞ Jeremiah ☜

When You Feel Forced to Serve

You are stronger than I am, and you have
overpowered me.

JEREMIAH 20:7

hen I was an adjunct instructor in Bible literature, I often read aloud portions of whatever book we were studying. Sometimes I did this to help
the students grasp the flavor of the document and other
times to get their attention. Once, when we were studying
Jeremiah, I noticed the class was showing little interest,
so I read some of his confessions.[1] I thought the students
would be intrigued with Jeremiah's honesty—*You can say
that to God!* After reading several, I paused as I searched

103

for words. I wanted to explain to the mostly nonreligious students about the challenges of serving God. Seizing the moment, one student spoke up and said, "He's a whiner."

"What?"

"Jeremiah is a whiner."

Other students chimed in. They agreed. They said he needed to shut up and get on with doing what God wanted. Their opinion was, If God calls you to do something, then do it. There's no need to cry or complain.

I wondered how those students would have responded if God had called them. As they were making plans to be accountants, teachers, and business owners, how would they have felt if God had interrupted their lives? How would they have responded if God had asked of them what he asked of Jeremiah?

Jeremiah's Call

Jeremiah was an ordinary young citizen, probably around the age of my students, living in Anathoth near Jerusalem in the southern kingdom of Judah. He was a member of a priestly family, so he was assuming that he would also be a priest, carrying on the work of his elders. But God called, and everything changed. He said, "Jeremiah, I want you to be a prophet."

Judging by the huge sales of *The Purpose-Driven Life*, many people would be glad to learn God's specific purpose for their lives, but this was not true of Jeremiah. He resisted God's call. He did not see himself the way God saw him. He said, "Sovereign Lord, I don't know how to speak; I am too young" (Jer. 1:6).

God told Jeremiah not to say he was too young. He said, "Go to the people I send you to, and tell them everything

I command you to say. Do not be afraid of them, for I will be with you to protect you" (vv. 7–8).

The Lord touched his lips and said, "I am giving you the words you must speak" (v. 9). Then God gave Jeremiah the task of condemning the corrupt life and practices of God's people, of warning them about the consequences of their sin and idolatry, and of pleading with them to repent and turn to God.

Even though his heart wasn't in it, Jeremiah tried to complete the task God gave him, but no one wanted to hear his harsh messages. The people preferred the comforting messages of the false prophets, who were also on the scene. They reassured the people that they were God's people and reminded them that the temple was located in Jerusalem in Judah, so God wasn't going to let anything happen to them.

Consequently they didn't like what Jeremiah had to say. In an effort to keep Jeremiah quiet, the people mistreated him. Some cursed him and spit on him. His neighbors, his family, the false prophets, priests, and even his friends rejected him.

Besides being rejected, Jeremiah was poor and had to undergo severe physical deprivation to deliver his prophecies. He lived a lonely life because God didn't allow him to marry and socialize, so he didn't even have the support of a wife and children. Neither would God let him attend community gatherings, such as funerals and weddings. He stood alone as a man of God, warning the people that unless they repented and changed their ways, they would lose the land God had given them.

The mistreatment, the rejection, the loneliness, and the emotional strain of having to speak the truth discouraged Jeremiah and engulfed him in despair.

Jeremiah's Depression

In his book *What You Can Change and What You Can't*, Dr. Marty Seligman, a researcher and psychology professor, says that depression is the emotion that comes in the wake of helplessness, individual failure, and unrealized attempts to gain power.[2] That would certainly describe Jeremiah's situation.

Jeremiah felt helpless about his appointed role. Having a specific call from God can be tremendously energizing or terribly confining. If you've wondered for a long time what your purpose is, and then God clearly tells you, and the purpose seems to suit you, you feel free and alive. You wonder why you never figured this out for yourself long ago.

But if God's call interrupts your life, and what he asks doesn't fit who you are—or who you ever thought of being—you feel as though a vise were closing in on you. You see yourself as having no choice because it is you against God. Remembering that the potter has all the power over the clay, Jeremiah's attitude was, "You are stronger than I am, and you have overpowered me" (Jer. 20:7). He had no choice but to be a prophet.

Even after resigning himself to the role and with God's help, being a prophet was more than Jeremiah had bargained for. He got so tired of preaching about violence and destruction that he determined he would quit. But he discovered he couldn't, because that too was beyond his control. "Whenever I speak . . . Lord, I am ridiculed and scorned all the time because I proclaim your message. But when I say, 'I will forget the Lord and no longer speak in his name,' then your message is like a fire burning deep within me. I try my best to hold it in, but can no longer keep it back" (vv. 8–9).

Jeremiah was a failure in that the object of his efforts was never achieved. No converts came forward. No one fell down on his knees in repentance. No one ever said, "You are right, Jeremiah. We should be heeding your advice." Instead, everyone in the land—the kings of Judah, the officials, the priests, and the people—were all against him. He took their criticisms to heart. Instead of seeing that the people were rejecting God, he took it personally. They were rejecting him.

Jeremiah never wanted power for power's sake. But if you are called to preach, then sometime or another you would like to know that your preaching is effective, that someone is getting it. Jeremiah was a powerful speaker and an excellent poet. He also acted out many symbolic messages to make his point. He was a clear and direct communicator with a compelling message, but if you judge power by results, there was no power in what he said. Consistently and passionately Jeremiah preached, but lives were not changed.

Because he was feeling helpless, experiencing failure, and being ineffective, it is a wonder that Jeremiah was able to carry on with being a prophet, but he did. He was faithful to the task. Perhaps the whining helped him. Unlike my students, I happen to believe in the value of whining. As that prolific writer, Anonymous, once said, "Why should I suffer in silence when I can still moan, wail, and complain?"

The Value of Whining

When I say I believe whining is valuable, I'm not advocating whining all the time or whining about everything. What

I believe is that complaining to God is beneficial when dealing with depression. It is a form of honest prayer.

Jesus taught me that I can be honest with God. Being a student of prayer, I've been particularly interested in Jesus' prayer life. Because I had studied his prayers, they imprinted themselves on my soul without my even realizing it. When I was recovering from depression and the physical symptoms were gone, a spiritual residue remained. Some of it was unforgiveness, but I was also uncertain about what God was doing—or not doing!—in our lives.

Bob and I had tried hard to be conscientious in following him. Bob had taken the jobs he lost after much prayer and deliberation. I couldn't figure out what God was doing in our lives, although I sure tried! He had disappointed me, and my brooding kept the hurt alive. I had to find a way to relieve the hurt, and that's when I instinctively knew to pray Jesus' honest prayer, "My God, my God, why have you forsaken me?" Only my version was, "How could you do it to us? How could you treat us this way?"

I was surprised by the strong emotion that tumbled out as I prayed, and that's one reason I recommend that depressed people whine—or even wail—to God. Few of the people we know would be able to handle such honesty and raw emotion, and yet we need to release it. So it's best to give it to God who already knows how we are feeling. We may shock our friends but we cannot shock God.

Jeremiah knew that. He was honest with God about how he felt and what he was thinking. "Although Jeremiah's complaints were numerous and vociferous, it is remarkable that these were always directed to God, not to man. Whatever problems were his, he did not take them to his neighbor but to God."[3]

108

He unzipped his inner self and let everything out when he prayed. There wasn't any pretense in the way he approached God—nothing that said, "I've got to dress up before I approach God." Neither did he feel the need to sort out his jumbled, often conflicting thoughts before he prayed.

- He wanted to serve God, but he didn't want to.
- He was unhappy, yet he was happy; sometimes he even expressed both emotions in the same prayer.
- At times he delighted in God, yet he also accused God of being unreliable.
- He felt compassion for the people, weeping and grieving over their behavior. But at other times he was hostile and vindictive toward them. In one scathing tirade to God, he asked that the worst of calamities should befall his enemies and their families because of their plots against him (Jer. 18:19–23).

In his prayers, Jeremiah fretted over his own personal troubles and what he had to endure, exaggerating his misery. Like Job, he rued the day he was born. Jeremiah pronounced a curse on the day and on the man who informed his father of his birth. Such sad news should have been suppressed, he said, not broadcast!

When he compared his situation to that of others—a tendency of people prone to depression—Jeremiah noticed his enemies were rich and prospered, while he was poor. This was grossly unfair! He said:

Lord . . . I must question you about matters of justice. Why are the wicked so prosperous? Why do dishonest people succeed? . . . They always speak well of you, yet they do not really care about you. But, Lord, you know me; you see what I do and how I love you. Drag these evil people away like sheep to be butchered; guard them until it is time for them to be slaughtered.

12:1–3

Jeremiah reminded God of how obedient he had been. "You spoke to me, and I listened to every word . . . I did not spend my time with other people, laughing and having a good time. In obedience to your orders I stayed by myself" (15:16–17). As he reminded God of how conscientious he had been, he was filled with anger. "Why do I keep on suffering? Why are my wounds incurable? Why won't they heal? Do you intend to disappoint me like a stream that goes dry in the summer?" (v. 18).

His lament released the continual tension he was experiencing and diminished the destructive power of the rumblings that churned and agitated within, plus it cleaned out his inner space so God could respond to him, which is another reason we need to be honest with God.

Divine Responses to Despair

Sometimes God just listened to Jeremiah, letting him speak his heart, letting him gain relief; but other times he made significant responses to Jeremiah's complaints—significant in the sense that they aided Jeremiah's recovery. This helps us see that often recovery requires more than whining.

God reassured Jeremiah that eventually his enemies would be punished. He said, "I have set a time for bringing disaster on the people of Anathoth, and when that time comes, none of them will survive" (Jer. 11:23).

110

The fact that his enemies would eventually get their just deserts didn't satisfy Jeremiah. He went on complaining. He wondered, Is God truly in command in his world? If the lot of the righteous is difficult, the way of the transgressor should be harder. Yet the opposite appeared to be true.

God did not answer directly these concerns; rather he confronted Jeremiah with the deeper implications of his call. This was no time to become discouraged, for the long haul was yet ahead. In effect, the Lord said, "Jeremiah, if you think things have been bad up to this point, then cheer up—they will get much worse!" In other words, there is a time to quit complaining and get on with doing what needs to be done. While whining is beneficial, it is not to go on forever.

As Jeremiah continued to preach of Judah's doom (15:1–9), he saw God as being unfair and bemoaned his fate (vv. 10, 15–18). He was the good person, the obedient person, but he was ridiculed and threatened. People wanted to kill him.

At that, God insisted that Jeremiah repent. He said to Jeremiah:

> If you return, I will take you back, and you will be my servant again. If instead of talking nonsense you proclaim a worthwhile message, you will be my prophet again. The people will come back to you, and you will not need to go to them. I will make you like a solid bronze wall as far as they are concerned. They will fight against you, but they will not defeat you. I will be with you to protect you and keep you safe. I will rescue you from the power of wicked and violent people.
>
> verses 19–21

Jeremiah had often called on people to repent and return to God. Now God was asking him to repent if he was going to be a true prophet. He must "utter what is precious, and not what is worthless" if he is to be God's voice (v. 19 RSV). Rather than bemoaning the treatment he was receiving, Jeremiah must rise above complaining and start proclaiming the valuable truth of God.

Through repenting and changing his focus to what was precious, a shift took place within Jeremiah so that he eventually became a fortified wall of bronze that could not be defeated. Repenting and changing focus didn't negate the value of his honest confessions. Fortification was a process, and whining was a part of it in which he opened himself to God and gave him a way to respond. Through honest praying and God's answers, Jeremiah found his way out of the darkness that had engulfed him for so long. He went from being a prophet of despair to being a prophet of hope.

From Despair to Hope

Hope was born out of Jeremiah's pain and agony. His complaints ceased as if he had finally come to terms with his call and its challenges.[4] Through honest prayer, the perplexed man of God found peace and strength and became a prophet of hope.

- Jeremiah bought a field in his hometown of Anathoth just as the Babylonians were about to overrun the country and take the Judeans captive. Jeremiah was a bachelor and had no need of a farm, yet he saw beyond the deportation and bought the field as an act of faith that houses, fields, and vineyards would again be bought in Judah.

112

- Jeremiah wrote to the people of Judah who were captured and taken to Babylon. He gave them God's reassuring words: "I alone know the plans I have for you,
plans to bring you prosperity and not disaster, plans to
bring about the future you hope for. . . . I will restore
you to your land. . . . I will bring you back to the land
from which I had sent you away into exile" (Jer. 29:11,
14).

- He encouraged those going into exile to set up signs
and mark the road so they could find their way back
(31:21). Jeremiah promised the disheartened Judeans
that God would always be open to restoring them to
their land if they repented.

- Jeremiah described a new covenant that God would
initiate. The time would come when God would make
a new covenant with the people of Judah. It would
not be like the covenant that he had made with
Moses and the Israelites, a covenant they had not
kept. The new covenant would be written on their
hearts (vv. 31–33).

- As the Judeans surveyed the ravaged Jerusalem after
the Babylonians had destroyed it, Jeremiah offered an
optimistic view of the city's future. He encouraged those
left in the ravaged city that one day the streets would
"hear again the shouts of gladness and joy and the happy
sounds of wedding feasts" (33:10–11). Jeremiah was
confident God would make the land as prosperous as
it had been before, including a rebuilt temple.

Jeremiah's prophecies of hope are cited repeatedly in later
biblical books (see 2 Chron. 36:21–33; Ezra 1:1–3; Dan. 9:2),
showing how crucial his words were. His prophecies gave
God's people encouragement to maintain their faith while

they were in exile until they returned to Israel, which finally happened when the Persians defeated the Babylonians.

His legacy of hope continues beyond Judah's exile and return to Jerusalem to help us in the twenty-first century.

What We Can Learn

From Jeremiah's struggle and resolution, we can find help for walking out of darkness when it engulfs us.

Be Honest with God

To Jeremiah prayer was not just a matter of petitioning or thanking God. It was an intimate sharing of the soul. Whatever his tensions, he brought them to God. There he discovered that the Lord was a sympathetic listener and that God wouldn't back off or refuse to hear certain things. He wouldn't gasp in surprise, and he wouldn't say, "I would never have believed that about you." We can be honest with God.

Examine Your Life

Jeremiah's conversations with God remind us that sometimes repentance may be needed as a part of the soul work we need to do to get over being depressed. Jeremiah had a difficult way to go, a way that any person would find difficult, but that doesn't mean he was completely innocent. Jeremiah was right, but he was also wrong.

As we think about what led to our depression, we usually see ourselves as heroes. Whatever trouble we have, it is someone else's fault. But at times, for recovery's sake or growth's sake, it may be beneficial to ask, *Could I be at fault here in any way?* If the answer is yes, then repentance may be necessary to find light in the darkness.

Be Encouraged

Jeremiah's example of endurance can encourage us. From the time that God called him, Jeremiah stood alone, declaring God's message of doom and weeping over the fate of his beloved country. It never got easy; still, he did what God wanted. He was faithful for forty years to the task God called him to do. During that time Jeremiah never received the "Prophet of the Year" award, but he got a bronze medal for endurance (see Jer. 1:18).

Jeremiah valiantly pressed on even when he was depressed. During those times of complaining, times when he couldn't see the light in the darkness, he was still faithful to the task. He shows us we can be God's servants even when we are depressed, if we remain faithful. His wailing and weeping was a part of a fortification process so that he became the bronze wall that God promised him he would be. He became the wall that could not be defeated.

Replay and Reflect

How would you respond if God interrupted your life?

Why would a person struggle with God's call? Why not feel blessed instead of stressed?

Have you ever felt as keenly as Jeremiah that life was unfair? What did you see as being unfair?

Have you ever complained to God as honestly as Jeremiah did? What was God's response?

How can a person not know that he or she needs to repent?

Why continue with a difficult task if there are no rewards?

8

◄| Jonah |►

When Anger Brews

I have every right to be angry—angry
enough to die!

JONAH 4:9

*L*ike Jeremiah, Jonah was going about his day-to-day
activities when God interrupted his life. Jonah was
a prophet who was committed to advising the king and
speaking for God to the nation of Israel. One day God
startled Jonah. He said, "Go to Nineveh, that great city,
and speak out against it" (Jon. 1:2).

Unless you have ever tied your faith to a certain area—
and we may do this unconsciously—you can't understand
what a jolt God's words were to Jonah! When I was in sem-

inary in Texas, my friends and I often discussed what we were going to do after we graduated. We wondered if God wanted us to serve him in a foreign country, a particular U.S. state, a rural location, or a big city. After we explored various possibilities, Judy, a Texan, would say, "I'll do anything God wants me to do; I'll go anywhere he wants me to go, as long as it's in the state of Texas." She would smile as she said it, and the rest of us would laugh, but we all knew she was dead serious.

Israel was Jonah's Texas. He had never considered the possibility that God would call him to prophesy anywhere else, especially some place like Nineveh.

Oh, No, Not Nineveh!

First, Jonah resisted going to Nineveh because it was Gentile territory. The Israelites considered themselves spiritually superior to Gentiles, so it would be beneath Jonah to go and preach to them. It would be a demotion.

Another reason Jonah resisted going to Nineveh was because it was the capital of Assyria, a ruthless, wicked empire on the rise. As the Assyrians conquered country after country, they treated subjugated peoples with extreme cruelty. They were a people to be feared. Eventually the Assyrians would conquer tiny Israel, but when Jonah was prophesying, Israel was politically secure and spiritually smug. They saw themselves as superior to Gentiles and to the wicked Assyrians.

Jonah didn't say a word in response to God's call, but you can imagine what was going through his mind: *God, you've got to be kidding. You want me to go into Gentile territory? None of the other prophets you called had to go outside Israel to speak to the uncircumcised. Just the thought grosses me* out. *Besides, these people are so evil; they don't deserve any kind of message from you. We're your people, not those wicked Assyrians. Well, I'm not going. I'm getting out of here!*

Jonah set out in the opposite direction from Nineveh to get away from the Lord (Jon. 1:3). He went to Joppa, a seacoast town, where he found a ship about to go to Tarshish. He paid his fare, went aboard, and sailed with the crew, but he soon learned you can run but you can't hide from God.

God of Land *and* Sea

Once Jonah was aboard ship, God "sent a great wind on the sea" (Jon. 1:4 NIV). A violent storm arose and threatened to break up the ship. Even the seasoned sailors on board were afraid. Each prayed to his god to be saved. Then they frantically threw cargo into the sea to lighten the ship, to keep it from being destroyed.

Jonah went below deck. He "lay down and fell into a deep sleep" (v. 5 NIV). This was odd behavior for someone on a ship that was tossing and turning, threatening to break apart at any minute. How could he sleep at a time like this? Didn't he care about the fate of the others? Didn't he care about himself? Wasn't he frightened?

The captain found his behavior to be incredible. He roused Jonah and said, "How can you sleep? Get up and call on your god!" (v. 6 NIV). If he wasn't willing to help, the least he could do was pray.

Jonah responded to the captain's admonition with a stony silence. Like a stubborn child who has been reprimanded, he was unwilling to admit any wrongdoing. A child crosses his arms, locks his body, glares at you, and refuses to move. He doesn't say anything, but his glare speaks for him. It says,

You can't make me admit I was wrong. I'm not a bit sorry, and I'm not moving. I'm not about to cooperate with you.

To withdraw from the others, to be alone during a raging storm, to ignore the commotion on board, not to be struck by fear the way the others were, to fall into a deep sleep and not respond to the captain *may* indicate that Jonah was depressed. Since we know so little about Jonah at this point, we have to assume that if he was depressed it was due to God's asking him to go to Nineveh. But why would a person be depressed over a specific request from God?

Life Interrupted

Jonah had a life that suited him—a life in which he was serving God—and a work he could take pride in. Then God stepped in and asked him to do something not only out of his comfort zone but actually repulsive to him. Jonah was humiliated by the idea of being a prophet to Gentile Assyrians, so he attempted to escape God's directive. He responded by running away and withdrawing.

Without thinking it through, Jonah took a ship to Tarshish. Perhaps he assumed that if he could get out of Israel—out of the land he associated with God's presence—the voice of God would stop urging him to go to Nineveh. It was a quick, emotional response and then when he was on ship, reality sunk in. He realized he had cut himself off from the role that meant so much to him, and besides, he was in Gentile territory! He hadn't solved a thing by running away. While earlier he had wondered what God was thinking, now he wondered, *What was I thinking?*

Angry with God and down on himself and yet not wanting the pain of dealing with either, he went below deck and slept. A depressed person experiences a change in sleep patterns. Usually he or she is unable to sleep or sleeps much less than normal; however, a small percentage of people will oversleep. It is a compelling sleep and often a welcome sleep to avoid the pain of reality. When you're asleep you don't have to comply, respond, react, or make choices.

While Jonah slept below deck, the sailors took action. They "said to each other, 'Come, let us cast lots to find out who is responsible for this calamity.' They cast lots and the lot fell on Jonah" (Jon. 1:7 NIV).

Then they confronted Jonah. "Tell us," they insisted. "What have you done to cause this awful storm? Why have you caused us so much trouble? What do you do? Where do you come from? What is your country? What is your nationality?"

Wisely, this time Jonah didn't remain silent. He said, "I am a Hebrew and I worship the LORD, the God of heaven, who made the sea and the land" (v. 9 NIV).

"You worship who?" The men were terrified. "Your God is the God of heaven who made this sea?" Aghast at the ramifications of this, they asked, "What have you done?"

All the while, the sea was getting rougher and rougher. So the sailors asked Jonah, "What should we do to make the sea calm down?" (v. 11 NIV).

"'Pick me up and throw me into the sea,' he replied, 'and it will become calm'" (v. 12 NIV). He knew that the terrible storm had occurred because of him.

The sailors hesitated. They really hated to throw a man overboard, so they tried their best to row back to land, but they just couldn't do it, for the sea grew even wilder.

Then they prayed, "'O LORD, please do not let us die for taking this man's life. Do not hold us accountable for killing an innocent man, for you, O LORD, have done as you pleased.' Then they took Jonah and threw him overboard, and the raging sea grew calm" (vv. 14–15 NIV).

The external storm stopped, but not Jonah's internal storm, not that it was going to matter since death by drowning seemed likely. Spiraling downward, he was in such great distress that he called to God for help, and God answered. That's when Jonah's petulance turned to joy.

Jonah's Joy

God loved Jonah so much that he arranged for a great fish to swallow him. Jonah was filled with gratitude. While earlier he had seemed listless and uncaring regarding his life ("Throw me into the sea," he had said), his attitude changed when he met death face-to-face. With relief, he marveled at his spectacular rescue and prayed an eloquent, emotional prayer inside the fish. He spoke with God about what he had been experiencing and how relieved he was to be rescued.

> From the depths of death I called, and Lord, you heard me! You threw me into the ocean depths; I sank down into the floods of waters and was covered by your wild and stormy waves. . . . I sank beneath the waves, and death was very near. The waters closed above me; the seaweed wrapped itself around my head. I went down to the bottoms of the mountains that rise from off the ocean floor. I was locked out of life and imprisoned in the land of death. But, O Lord my God, you have snatched me from the yawning jaws of death!
>
> Jonah 2:2–3, 5–6 TLB

Jonah described his experience in graphic and horrifying detail. Can you imagine the choking sensation, being closed in, entangled in seaweed? Can you sense Jonah's panic as he felt imprisoned in the land of death?

Death had seemed imminent and inevitable to Jonah. He was certain he was going to die, but he didn't. God rescued him by providing a great fish to swallow Jonah, keep him alive, and then take him to dry land. Jonah was grateful for God's deliverance and pledged his faithfulness: "Those who cling to worthless idols forfeit the grace that could be theirs. But I, with a song of thanksgiving, will sacrifice to you. What I have vowed I will make good. Salvation comes from the LORD" (vv. 8–9 NIV).

You would think that, after such an unusual encounter, such a dramatic rescue, such a grateful prayer, and such a firm commitment, Jonah would no longer struggle with depression or God's leadership, but the rest of his story shows otherwise.

God again told him to go to Nineveh. This time Jonah obliged. He went to Nineveh, but his heart still wasn't in it. The stubborn inner child that wouldn't open his mouth muttered under his breath the entire distance to Nineveh and kicked every loose stone in his path.

Jonah felt no compassion for Nineveh's spiritual problems, but he did what God wanted. He preached. He shouted to the people: "Forty days from now Nineveh will be destroyed!" (3:4 TLB).

Nineveh was so large that it took three days to walk through it. Jonah was expecting to preach at least that long, but on the first day, the people repented! Despite the wickedness of the Ninevite people, they were receptive to God's message. The people, including the king, responded by fasting, praying, and giving up their evil ways.

"God saw what they did; he saw that they had given up their wicked behavior. So he changed his mind and did not punish them as he had said he would" (v. 10). This embarrassed Jonah. What he said would happen wasn't going to happen. A prophet's prophecy was not going to come true! That's when Jonah's joy turned to complaint.

Jonah's Complaint

Most speakers would be elated that people heeded their message and changed. Jeremiah would have been delighted, but Jonah was disappointed. He "was greatly displeased and became angry" (Jon. 4:1 NIV).

Seeing thousands of Ninevites repenting and turning to God enraged Jonah. He wanted God to confine his love and mercy to Israel. He pouted when his message of doom did not come true. Even though God had been merciful to him, he could not handle the thought of God having mercy on evil Gentiles. It just wasn't right. His anger spilled forth in an honest prayer: "O Lord, is this not what I said when I was still at home? That is why I was so quick to flee to Tarshish. I knew that you are a gracious and compassionate God, slow to anger and abounding in love, a God who relents from sending calamity. Now, O Lord, take away my life, for it is better for me to die than to live" (vv. 2–3 NIV).

If we had any doubts about his being depressed, we don't now. Jonah's misery has progressed to the point that he is once again suicidal. He doesn't care whether he lives any longer. Angry and irrational, he asks God to take his life. His joy at being rescued from the swirling waters of the deep has been forgotten.

In most of the stories we have looked at—stories of Moses, Naomi, Job, and Elijah—I found it easy to be sympathetic. But not here.

If we've ever been depressed, we understand accumulated stress, loss, and exhaustion and can identify with Moses, Naomi, Job, and Elijah. We can understand their succumbing to despair, but it is hard to identify with Jonah who pouts because God is loving, merciful, patient, and kind. How can we be sympathetic with someone like that? Don't you want to say, "Jonah, get a grip!"

If we had been able to say this to Jonah, it probably wouldn't have helped. Telling a depressed person to snap out of it or get a grip usually only reinforces his or her grievance. God chose a better approach to help Jonah. Without condemning him, God questioned Jonah about his anger and gave him an object lesson to challenge his thinking and change his feelings.

Questions and a Plant

When you are depressed over things that others may consider petty or irrational, as Jonah was, it is hard to get beyond your depressed feelings, because you are reluctant to say what is bothering you. It seems right and reasonable to you to feel the way you do, but you hesitate to talk about it. You have a sense that someone will challenge you if you admit your feelings, so you keep quiet. You don't want someone's rational explanation of why you shouldn't feel the way you do. You don't want to argue. You want to hold on to your thinking just the way it is, without logic applied to your pain.

But not talking about what is bothering you stands in the way of your recovery. You rob yourself of the healthy option of getting your despair out in the open where it loses power and can be dealt with. Your unexpressed emotions hinder your ability to communicate with God and provide a hot-house for growing depression. When Jonah expressed his feelings to God, God was able to respond and help him.

God asked Jonah, "Have you any right to be angry?" (Jon. 4:4 NIV). There it was, out in the open. The basic underlying cause of his depression—anger—was identified and labeled.

The Interpreter's Bible says, "'Have you any right to be angry?' may also be translated, 'Are you very angry?' suggesting a gentleness and pity on the part of God toward Jonah, as a parent might speak to a sulking child."[1] It wasn't a "You ought" or "You should" but a "We're going to work this out" approach.

The question was asked, and the label applied, but Jonah, being the stubborn person that he was, resisted answering. If he did, he might have to relinquish his way of thinking. Jonah preferred to continue to mull over the situation, so he withdrew from the city.

He made a leafy shelter for himself and sat in its shade, waiting to see what would happen to Nineveh. Brooding under what little shade his shelter provided, he clung to the hope that destruction would still come to the city. God had sent him to pronounce judgment on Nineveh, to witness its repentance, and to rejoice in its salvation. But Jonah chose to sit alone, nursing his hurt feelings, singing the blues, and hoping for the city's destruction.

When the leaves of the shelter withered in the heat, God mercifully arranged for a plant to grow up quickly. The plant spread its broad leaves over Jonah's head to shade him and make him more comfortable. "Jonah was very happy about the vine" (v. 6 NIV). Perhaps he felt that the vine was a blessing from God, a confirmation that things were going to turn out the way he wanted. Hope flared within him that Nineveh would still be destroyed.

But at dawn the next day, God provided a worm—here comes the object lesson! The worm attacked the vine so that it withered. There went his shade! Then a hot wind also came from the east, adding to Jonah's discomfort. As the sun beat on his head, he thought he was going to faint. He was so miserable he wished he could die. He concluded, "It would be better for me to die than to live" (v. 8 NIV).

All the emotional events he had been through—the major ones and the minor ones—weighed heavily on him and were compounded by the heat. It was just too much. There wasn't any point in going on.

The plant that God destroyed—the plant that Jonah was so happy about—gave Jonah a taste of what destruction was like. He found the taste bitter, but he didn't compassionately connect that lesson with the inhabitants of Nineveh. He had no empathy for them; instead, his focus was on the plant. He was angry about the plant's demise.

God asked Jonah another question: "What right do you have to be angry about the plant?" Jonah replied, "I have every right to be angry—angry enough to die!" (v. 9).

He was angry enough to die over a wilted plant! His anger was far out of proportion to the reason, but at least he admitted how angry he was. He acknowledged the problem. He was honest about the intensity of his anger, and his honesty gave God further room to communicate with him. It was time for some "truth talk."

Facing the Truth

"The Lord said to him, 'This plant grew up in one night and disappeared the next; you didn't do anything for it and you didn't make it grow—yet you feel sorry for it!'" (Jon. 4:10). Jonah did nothing to deserve the plant; it was a gift from God. It was given to him without any effort on his part. Furthermore, the plant was fragile and its usefulness was limited. It perished almost as quickly as it had grown. Yet Jonah placed great value on such a fragile plant and pitied it when it died.

"Jonah," he went on, "let's get things in perspective. Do you really think I shouldn't spare Nineveh? With your attitude, you're putting one plant on the same level as 120,000 innocent children, as well as many animals. Can you really compare the two? Surely, infants and beasts rate higher on your scale of values than plants—or don't they?" (see v. 11).

How did Jonah respond to God's final questions and object lesson? Did he remain angry and unrepentant? Did he hold on to his depression and take his own life? Did he go back to Israel feeling disgraced? Or did he learn to appreciate the breadth of God's grace?

I can't answer these questions because the book of Jonah leaves us hanging about Jonah's response and future. Perhaps that is so we would ask ourselves some questions.

Am I like Jonah?

James R. Edwards, who wrote about Jonah in his book *The Divine Intruder*, said:

> Suppose you were to die tonight and go to heaven. Would there be anyone you would be grieved to see there? The office partner who got the promotion you thought you deserved, even though he was phony as a form letter? The undeserving kid who got the full-tuition scholarship you worked so hard for? The spouse who betrayed you? The unscrupulous real estate agent who defrauded you? The

debtor who refused to pay up? Don't laugh too quickly at Jonah's tirade against grace. He is not alone.[2]

We all would benefit from thinking about how we may be acting like Jonah. Are we upset by the grace shown to others?

Can I Acknowledge Anger?

In *Healing for Damaged Emotions*, a book that has helped many Christians, David A. Seamands wrote: "If you have a consistently serious problem with depression, you have not resolved some area of anger in your life. As surely as the night follows the day, depression follows unresolved, repressed, or improperly expressed anger."[3]

Seamands also said that the most concise definition of depression he knew was "frozen rage," which may explain Jonah's silence. He was angry from the time God called him, but he kept his anger pushed down. No wonder that when he finally admitted it, he was angry enough to die.

What Happened to Jonah?

This may not seem like an important question, but I believe it is. Your answer says something about you. Are you optimistic and hopeful? Do you believe God is compassionate? Do you believe God cares about us even when we are petulant and disagreeable? Or are you pessimistic? Do you believe we can get to a point that we are beyond redemption?

I believe God's final recorded words to Jonah softened his stubborn heart, melted his anger, and sent him back to Israel a changed man. I believe this because God has challenged and changed me many times.

When I was in seminary—where my friend said she would go anywhere God wanted her to go, just not out of Texas—I was a Jonah, running away from God's call. Like Jonah my theology was faulty. His theology said God loved only the chosen people, and mine said if God wants you to do something, it will probably be something you won't enjoy.

I'm glad to say that Jonah and I were both proven wrong. Jonah learned that God loves Gentiles, and I learned that serving God is a joy. There have been other times too, such as when I was depressed and my thinking was challenged. Each time I learned something new about God, or I came to know him better. Because of these experiences I have a bias. I believe Jonah returned to Israel a changed man. How about you? If there had been another verse to the book of Jonah, what do you think it would have said?

Replay and Reflect

How were the questions significant that the sailors asked Jonah?

With what part of Jonah's story do you identify?

His running away

His prayer

His pouting

His anger

Have you ever known anyone to complain about God always being patient, always kind, and always ready to change his mind? What kinds of situations might a person be in to complain about the patience and kindness of God or accuse him of changing his mind?

Do you want God to behave as the God you have always pictured in your mind or do you want your knowledge of him expanded?

Is your behavior consistent with what you believe or are you grieved by the grace shown to others?

Why would a person keep his or her anger inside rather than express it?

9

⊰| Solomon |⊱

When Cynicism Sets In

Everything leads to weariness—a weariness too great for words.

ECCLESIASTES 1:8

*A*ndrew Solomon, author of an atlas on depression, wrote that depression is the most cynical
thing in the world.[1] We have a prime example of this in the
depression of King Solomon. I find it odd that this would be
the case since he was a very wise man: "Solomon's wisdom
was greater than the wisdom of all the men of the East,
and greater than all the wisdom of Egypt. He was wiser
than any other man" (1 Kings 4:30–31 NIV).

Solomon was also a man who experienced great personal
success and was very wealthy. He wielded tremendous

power as king of Israel. With his great wealth, he was able to enjoy the finer things of life, pursuing many kinds of pleasurable activities. Sounds like a man who had everything, doesn't it?

Well, at one time in his life he didn't, as Ecclesiastes, one of his major writings, illustrates.[2] Something was missing, something that Solomon looked for and didn't find.

The Pursuit

Solomon pursued wisdom, knowledge, pleasure, and wealth in seeking a meaningful life. He earnestly studied and explored all that was done under heaven and succeeded in gaining wisdom. He said, "I have grown and increased in wisdom more than anyone who has ruled over Jerusalem before me" (Eccles. 1:16 NIV). "God gave Solomon wisdom and very great insight, and a breadth of understanding as measureless as the sand on the seashore" (1 Kings 4:29 NIV).

With similar earnestness, Solomon plunged into a life of pleasure, madness, and folly (see Eccles. 1:17; 2:1, 12). He "wanted to see what was worthwhile for men to do under heaven during the few days of their lives" (2:3 NIV). He spared no expense in pursuing wine, women, and song. He said, "I denied myself nothing my eyes desired; I refused my heart no pleasure" (v. 10 NIV).

With equal energy, he worked hard. He built buildings and planted vineyards. He did things on a large scale, amassing a fortune and living in luxury.

> I undertook great projects: I built houses for myself and planted vineyards. I made gardens and parks and planted all kinds of fruit trees in them. I made reservoirs to water groves of flourishing trees. I bought male and female slaves

and had other slaves who were born in my house. I also owned more herds and flocks than anyone in Jerusalem before me. I amassed silver and gold for myself, and the treasure of kings and provinces. I acquired men and women singers, and a harem as well—the delights of the heart of man. I became greater by far than anyone in Jerusalem before me.

verses 4–9 NIV

When Solomon stopped, looked back, and analyzed all that he had accomplished, he realized that all his effort had been for nothing (v. 11). With wisdom came sadness. "For with much wisdom comes much sorrow; the more knowledge, the more grief" (1:18 NIV). He tasted pleasure and could only conclude that laughter is foolish (see 2:2). Neither was meaning gained from all his hard work. When he surveyed all that his hands had done and what he had toiled to achieve, he concluded: "Everything was meaningless . . . nothing was gained under the sun" (2:11 NIV).

Wisdom, pleasure, wealth, and success failed to give Solomon the fulfillment he longed for and consequently, he sang the blues.

Solomon's Song

Solomon sang his blues to a young person, probably a student of wisdom. His song had a repetitive chorus: "Vanity of vanities, all is vanity" (Eccles. 1:2 NKJV). *Vanity* means emptiness, uselessness, or worthlessness, so to sing, "Vanity of vanities," is like saying, "Life is *really* empty" or "Life is useless, all useless" (TEV) or "Utterly meaningless!" (NIV).

This superlative expression reveals Solomon's bleak outlook on life. No wonder he encouraged his young student to enjoy life while he could before the years would pass, and he too would say, "I don't enjoy life" (see 11:9–12:1). That's where Solomon was—in a place of no longer enjoying life, a prime characteristic of depression.

Besides having a repetitive chorus, he also had a repetitive phrase: "chasing after the wind" (see 1:14; 2:11, 17, 26). "Chasing after the wind" was Solomon's way of expressing the futility of his efforts. Who can catch the wind and hold it? You may clutch at it, but when you open your hand, it will be gone and your hand will be empty. From here Solomon began to overgeneralize. Not only were his efforts futile, but so was life. It had no meaning either (see 3:19).

Feeling that whatever you do doesn't matter can lead to depression or be a symptom of depression. In Solomon's case, both may be true. As Solomon examined life after pursuing wisdom, pleasure, and wealth, he concluded that it was futile to exert effort. This resulted in a "what's the use?" attitude. "You work and worry your way through life, and what do you have to show for it? As long as you live, everything you do brings nothing but worry and heartache. Even at night your mind can't rest. It is all useless" (2:22–23).

Another symptom of Solomon's depression was his preoccupation with death (see 2:16; 3:18–21; 7:1–2, 4; 9:13–15; 11:7–8). One commentator said Solomon had the gloomiest view of death of anyone in the Bible. One particularly bitter pill for Solomon to swallow was the realization that after death, a man is soon forgotten (see 2:16). It makes little difference whether he is a wise man or a fool. All remembrance of him will soon be wiped out. Like a dumb animal, man dies and is forgotten. How can life have meaning if it is to end in oblivion?

Solomon wrestled with life and death, doing and not doing, weeping and laughing, and fairness and unfairness.

He acknowledged there was a season for everything, but this didn't help. It only made man's existence even more perplexing, for he could not find out what God's purpose was in an "eternal round of events" (3:15).[3]

Solomon's young student may have had a hard time following what he was saying. (Many of us do when we read Ecclesiastes!) Solomon used different literary types, switching from prose to poetry and back again. He quoted wisdom sayings that didn't always connect with each other. He would leave a subject, go on to something else, and then come back to it. He also seemed to contradict himself on some things. For example, Solomon advised against pursuing pleasure for it was useless and meaningless. Yet he also encouraged enjoying the good life; he counseled his listener to eat, drink, and find enjoyment in life and work.

I wish I could resolve the confusing message of Ecclesiastes but I can't. What I can suggest, though, is an explanation. Solomon sounds like a ruminator, a person who spends a lot of time thinking and analyzing.

Rumblings of a Ruminator

If Solomon was a ruminator, his ability to synthesize and chew on observations and experiences probably contributed to his role as a wisdom teacher. It would have enabled him to study life, ponder his observations, and come to insightful conclusions that he passed on to others.

This would also explain why Ecclesiastes is disorganized and hard to follow. Until he has resolved what has happened and found a meaningful explanation or solution, a ruminator will usually keep coming back to what is pressing on his mind. His thoughts may even be contradictory or conflicting as he tries to figure things out.

A ruminator is prone to developing depression if he or she is a pessimist. You don't have to read much of Ecclesiastes to see that Solomon was a pessimist.

"What has happened before will happen again. What has been done before will be done again. There is nothing new in the whole world" (Eccles. 1:9).

"What is twisted cannot be straightened; what is lacking cannot be counted" (v. 15 NIV).

"Whatever happens or can happen has already happened before. God makes the same thing happen again and again" (3:15).

"We labor, trying to catch the wind, and what do we get? We get to live our lives in darkness and grief, worried, angry, and sick" (5:16–17).

"How can anyone know what is best for us in this short, useless life of ours—a life that passes like a shadow? How can we know what will happen in the world after we die?" (6:12).

Ruminating is a mental exercise, chewing things over in our thoughts, but if a good listener becomes available, we ruminators—yes, I'm one!—appreciate the opportunity to talk about what's bothering us. And Solomon, because he was a teacher, could command an audience. He was the one with authority! Teachers can take advantage of their students. Maybe you know this from experience when you sat under teachers who digressed from the subject and expounded on a topic perplexing to them. They may have given you the impression that it was for the good of the group or it was something you ought to be concerned about, but still you knew it was a personal issue. You may have sighed heavily, tapped your pencil, or doodled while you waited for the teacher to get back to the subject at hand.

At times we all ruminate. You may be doing a little right now, tapping your foot as you wonder how someone like Solomon could be depressed. You recognize his joyless spirit, the sadness, the gloomy pessimism, his somber thoughts on death, and his "what's the use?" attitude. What is harder to understand, though, is why he felt this way. Unfortunately, the reason is not as clear as it was in the lives of the other biblical characters we have studied. We don't know for sure; we can only wonder. Did it have something to do with where he was in life?

The View from the Middle

One commentator said Solomon must have been a young man when he wrote Ecclesiastes. She wrote that Ecclesiastes has "a tone of youthfulness."[4] Other commentators see him as an old man, mostly because of the way he described an old person in his advice to the young.

> So remember your Creator while you are still young, before those dismal days and years come when you will say, "I don't enjoy life." That is when the light of the sun, the moon, and the stars will grow dim for you, and the rain clouds will never pass away. Then your arms, that have protected you, will tremble, and your legs, now strong, will grow weak. Your teeth will be too few to chew your food, and your eyes too dim to see clearly. Your ears will be deaf to the noise of the street. You will barely be able to hear the mill as it grinds or music as it plays, but even the song of a bird will wake you from sleep. You will be afraid of high places, and walking will be dangerous. Your hair will turn

white; you will hardly be able to drag yourself along, and all desire will be gone.

Ecclesiastes 12:1–5

I don't see Solomon as young or old. I see him as somewhere in between. His descriptions of his pursuits of wisdom, pleasure, and success indicate that he had to have some years on him. This is a person who has lived a while.

But I don't think he was old. For one reason, his picture of old age is almost too dismal to have been written by an old person. When I researched midlife growth for a book I wrote, I learned that people in their middle years have a more dismal view of old age than people who are actually old! Thoughts and fears about aging are worse than aging itself.

Middle-agers are also more preoccupied with death than older people. One social scientist defines middle age as occurring when you start counting how many years you have left instead of how many years you have lived. Solomon, as noted above, was keenly aware of how much time he had left.

As they count the years they have left, middle-agers evaluate where they have been, which appears to be what Solomon was doing in Ecclesiastes. Looking back, Solomon recognized his achievements. He had acquired great wealth and had built palaces, government offices, and the temple in Jerusalem. He was an extraordinarily successful king who exerted great power. He had gained fame far and wide for his wisdom. When you think of what many people aim for in life, Solomon had those things. He had wealth, interesting work, power, fame, wisdom, influence, pleasure, and a huge family. In the eyes of many he had it all. He should have been happy but he wasn't. Something very important was missing. Life, he discovered, was "utterly meaningless!" (1:2 NIV).

Is Solomon overreacting? After all, he never knew stress to the degree Moses did, loss to the extent Job did, or rejection and ridicule as Jeremiah did. Why so melodramatic?

Don't underestimate how demoralizing the loss of meaning can be. I didn't realize the importance of purpose until it was gone. If anybody had told me prior to my depression how vital having a purpose is, it wouldn't have registered. In my earnestness in serving God, a sense of purpose had always just been there. When my husband got a job, after having been fired twice, I "went to work" mentally trying to make sense of what had happened. His new job was totally out of his field of interest, training, and calling. When I added up the years of training, Bob's work experiences, our prayers, and the fact that we had followed what we believed was God's leadership, it just didn't make sense. Because it didn't, I concluded that God did not have a purpose for my life. If that line of reasoning sounds illogical, it may have been. Ruminators don't always make sense.

I didn't know about ruminators at the time. Learning about that was one of the good things that came out of my interest in depression. If I had known, I might have been able to stop it, but I didn't. That's when I became depressed. There wasn't any reason after that to get up in the morning.

Without a purpose, you flounder and feel aimless. You just don't know what to do next, if anything. And you question whether anything would be worth the effort. There's no reason to go on with life.

A difficulty in struggling with a loss of purpose is that you can't talk it out because it is hard to find listeners who will be empathic. They say, "You don't believe God has a purpose for your life? You know better than that! Of course, he does." End of conversation.

No wonder Solomon ruminated out loud to a young student, and it was a worthwhile exercise. As he ranted and rumbled, insight came. After all he had experienced, after all he had observed, and after all he had chewed over, there was only one conclusion: "Have reverence for God, and obey his commands, because this is all that we were created for" (12:13). Here is Solomon's answer to the meaning of life: honoring God and walking in obedience. This also happens to be a remedy for depression.

Walking in the Light

Solomon's discovery reminds us that meaning is found in a personal relationship with God and in doing his will, but it also provides some helpful advice for getting over depression. That's because emotional reasoning plays a role in nearly all depressions.[5] Because things feel so negative to the depressed person, he or she assumes they truly are:

I feel abandoned by God, therefore I must be.

I feel inadequate, therefore I must be a worthless person.

I'm not in the mood to work, so I might as well stay in bed.

As you look at these statements, you know they are not true. No one is ever abandoned by God, and all people have worth in his eyes. The Bible has a lot to say about how and when to work, but it doesn't once stipulate that you have to be in the mood to work.

Honoring God and being obedient to what you know to be true breaks the power of emotional reasoning and can help a depressed person move out of darkness and walk in light.

If you are feeling abandoned by God, write on a card a verse that emphasizes God's faithfulness, such as, "Never will I leave you; never will I forsake you" (Heb. 13:5 NIV). Place it where you can see it, such as on your bathroom mirror, your refrigerator, or by your computer. Every time you look at it, read the verse out loud. Read it with emotion as if you were trying to convince someone else of its truth, and you will be surprised at the effect it will have on you over time.

To counter feelings of worthlessness, prepare a gift for a resident in a nursing home. Visit the person, give him or her the gift, and pray for the person. As the Bible says, "Pray for each other so that *you* may be healed" (James 5:16 NIV, italics added).

When you are not in the mood to work, say "This is the day the LORD has made" (Ps. 118:24 NIV), then make yourself get out of bed. Wash your face and do one job, even if it is cleaning out a drawer, shining the bathroom mirror, or sweeping the driveway. The feeling of accomplishment will elevate your mood some; the next day say the same thing and clean out two drawers. Little by little increase your efforts.

I realize some severely depressed persons may not be able to make these efforts, but they can recognize themselves as valued by God by calling a doctor and making an appointment to get help. Or they can ask a friend to make the appointment for them.

Being obedient is taking action—action that God wants us to take. The action will challenge the conclusions we've drawn from our emotional reasoning and give us some momentum in moving forward. I know because I had to do this to fully recover from depression.

Recognizing the Truth

After I sought professional help, the physical symptoms of depression ceased, and after I released my pent-up emotions to God, the dark cloud that hovered over me disappeared, but I still was listless about the future. The question of purpose remained. This was a spiritual problem: How could I bring my will in line with God's will and be obedient to the truth? I suppose there are many ways to do this, but I chose to do it through prayer.[6]

Tagged onto the loss of purpose was grief that our lives turned out as they had, lingering disappointment over Bob's new job, and anger at the way some believers had responded to us. Hopelessness about our future permeated my thinking as I kept being drawn back to the past. The hopelessness, the hurt, the grief, and the lack of belief in God's purpose—all had to go if I was to walk in the light. I chose to release these feelings through prayer: "Lord, I give you my hurts and my grief and my despair. I forgive the people who I believed hurt me. I give you the past. I release it to you."

Then I prayerfully affirmed living a purposeful life. "Today, Lord," I prayed, "I see myself as being free of depression and free of hurt. I see myself as feeling good about life again. I see you as smiling in approval of me because I remained faithful without understanding what was happening. I affirm my trust in you. I believe you have a purpose for me. I'm hopeful about the future."

The first morning I prayed this way, the effects of it lasted about one hour. Then I was back wallowing in self-pity and hurt. The next morning, I prayed again in the same way. This time, the effects lasted a little longer. Eventually, through prayerful release and affirmation, the day came when I was free of the trappings of the inner self, and I believed once again in the purpose of God. Then, and only

144

then, was I able to walk in light instead of darkness. Our circumstances had not changed, but I had.

The old hymn has it right. "Trust and obey for there's no other way to be happy in Jesus," and yet obeying can be so difficult. Even Solomon found it difficult.

When the Wise Was Not So Wise

Solomon, the wise teacher, turned to idols in the second half of his life, ignoring his own advice to honor and to obey God. He disobeyed God by marrying foreign wives, who brought their gods to Jerusalem. Solomon turned to worshiping idols, instead of the true God of Israel (1 Kings 11:4). Consequently, what he never found in chasing the wind continued to elude him as he chased other gods.

Meaning is found in reverencing and obeying God; it fulfills the purpose for which we were created. We feel in sync with him and feel that we are a part of something much larger than we can see and fully comprehend. When we step out in faith, trust God, and follow him, we can experience fullness and not emptiness.

Solomon could know the truth, even speak the truth to his student, and still not realize the full impact of what he was saying—at least not enough to make a difference in his life. How about you? As you waded through Solomon's dismal proclamations, listened to him ruminating, and noted his actions, what were your conclusions? What wisdom did you gain from your observations? Most important, do you believe obedience makes a difference?

Replay and Reflect

From your observations, what is the meaning of life?

Does the place where you are in life have any effect in making you depressed?

Why is having a sense of purpose so important?

Are our feelings always reliable?

How can a person walk in obedience when he or she doesn't feel like being obedient?

Why do you think Solomon could not follow his own advice?

10

⊰| A Psalmist |⊱

When the Loss Is Spiritual

As the deer pants for the water, so I long
for you, O God.

PSALM 42:1 TLB

*B*arbara really appreciated Sunday morning worship at her church; she looked forward to the
refreshment she experienced each week as she focused on
God. Then the worship leader resigned and left. A new one
was hired but his ability to lead wasn't the same. Musically
he was competent but he couldn't unite the worshipers
to sing as one voice and together focus on God. Barbara
missed that. The new leader seemed more interested in
perfecting the music rather than leading worship. Many

Sunday mornings, as she watched a "performance" on the platform, Barbara thought back to the way it used to be and wished it could be that way again.

As a single person, Marion had special times of worshiping alone. With no interruptions, she could take her time expressing herself and listening for God's responses. Her heart would swell with praise as she delighted in God's presence. Then she got married and children came, which was what she wanted, but amid the family noises and activity, Marion sometimes found herself hungry for lengthy times of solitary worship—times like the ones she used to have.

Tim reveled in a positive, upbeat worship environment at his church. The people clapped and raised their hands. There were drums, various musical instruments, and an electronic keyboard. They sang for long periods, and the pastor delivered powerful, motivating messages. The environment was so rich and so many people attended that Tim always experienced a power surge when he participated. As he left the building, he was ready to face the world, do anything God wanted. And then his reserve unit was activated, and Tim found himself worshiping in a tent in the desert. The chaplain was a kind person with a soft, monotone voice, and there were no musical instruments except one lone guitar. The service was a stark contrast to his former worship; there wasn't any power present. Tim left the tent feeling limp rather than recharged and also feeling homesick. He was homesick for a rich worship experience.

If you have had an experience similar to one of these, then you can understand the loss experienced by one of the psalmists. The author of Psalms 42 and 43 (originally the two formed a single composition) could no longer worship at the temple in Jerusalem, and he missed it terribly. He missed it enough that he became depressed over its loss.

Longing to Go Back

In Jerusalem he had gone with "the multitude, leading the procession to the house of God, with shouts of joy and thanksgiving among the festive throng" (Ps. 42:4 NIV). In the procession were singers and musicians, with maidens playing tambourines between them. Members of all the various tribes of Israel were present, and what a great time they had together as their voices united in a great paean to God! As they blessed God, the worshipers invited him to reveal his presence in the temple and declare his might, and he did. The psalmist had experienced this kind of worship, and he longed to experience it again. This longing was so intense that he compared it to that of a deer out of breath and thirsty: "As the deer pants for streams of water, so my soul pants for you, O God. My soul thirsts for God, for the living God" (vv. 1–2 NIV).

A picture in my sister's home portrays this scene. A group of grazing deer look up toward some mountains in which a waterfall cascades. Everything about the scene is beautiful, perfect, and serene. The picture, though, that the psalmist has in mind is "that of an animal of the chase, parched with thirst and panting for the one source of relief, the cool fresh water of ever-running streams."[1]

It is a thirst that the psalmist presumed could not be satisfied outside of Jerusalem; therefore, he assumed he might never experience it again because he was in exile. He was north of Jerusalem, far away from the holy hill where the temple was located. He was at Mount Mizar in the peaks of Hermon in the land of the Jordan.

Most of God's people at the time associated God's presence with the temple. It was the place where you experienced God. The psalmist figured if he wasn't in Jerusalem, then he couldn't experience the presence and good will of the living God. In Jordan he wondered, "When can I go and meet with God?" (v. 2 NIV). He wanted to go back to Jerusalem.

Having a worship experience that included processions, singers, musicians, and lots of people may have been especially important to the psalmist because he was a musician. The psalmist played the lyre (harp), and he was one of the Korahites, who were singers and musicians. They were renowned in King Jehoshaphat's day for singing and working together (see 2 Chron. 20:19). Psalms 42 and 43 were two of several psalms composed by the Korahite family (others are Psalms 44–49; 84–85; 87–88).

Making the psalmist's loss even more pronounced was the taunting of people around him—people he called foes and enemies. He described them as ungodly, deceitful, and wicked (43:1). They were godless men who mocked his faith (42:3, 10; 43:1–2).

These men could have been real enemies who had invaded Jerusalem and captured him, and that's how he ended up in Jordan. That's a possibility because we don't know how or why he ended up there.

Or his enemies could have been people living in Jordan who didn't understand his faith. As he pined away for what was left behind, perhaps the psalmist talked about his faith and God in grandiose terms, the way some people talk about the "good old days." As the people heard the psalmist go on and on, they wondered, *Where is this God who he declares is so mighty?* They wanted to see some evidence. The more the psalmist talked, the more they questioned him until all day long the men were saying, "Where is your God?" (42:3 NIV). Their questions and taunting magnified the Korahite's loss, resulting in his being sad and depressed.

The Downcast Soul

Four times the psalmist referred to himself as being depressed.

"Why am I so depressed?
Why this turmoil within me?" (42:5 HCSB).

"I am deeply depressed" (v. 6 HCSB).

"Why am I so depressed?
Why this turmoil within me?" (v. 11 HCSB).

"Why am I so depressed?
Why this turmoil within me?" (43:5 HCSB).

Instead of the word *depressed*, the New International Version uses *downcast*. The King James Version says *cast down*, which is, according to Phillip Keller, "an old English shepherd's term for a sheep that has turned over on its back and cannot get up again by itself."[2]

Keller, a shepherd and a writer, says that a fat or heavy sheep will lie down in some little hollow in the ground to get comfortable. If the sheep rolls over on its side to stretch out or to rest, the center of gravity of its body shifts. If the sheep turns on its back so far that its feet can no longer touch the ground, then it is difficult for it to get up again. The sheep panics and paws frantically. This only makes things worse, and it rolls over even farther. Now it is quite impossible for the sheep to get up by itself.

Lying on its back with its feet in the air, the sheep will sometimes bleat for help, but usually it lies there frightened and frustrated. As the gases build up and expand in the rumen, "they tend to retard and cut off blood circulation to extremities of the body, especially the legs."[3] The cast-down sheep is immobilized and helpless and if not rescued could die in a matter of hours. The sheep needs a shepherd to pick it up and set its feet on solid ground.

From this description, you can see why *cast down* is a good term to describe the depressed psalmist. He was in a hole and couldn't get up. He needed help. He needed a shepherd to reach for his hand and pull him out. He needed God, and so he prayed an honest prayer.

Or you could say he sang the blues. The Psalms were sung and they expressed deep feelings. Psalms 42 and 43 were called laments, and laments are the Bible's version of the blues.

The Lament

The blues is a unique form of music developed in this country in the late 1800s, but in a sense people have always sung the blues. The music form may have been different, but one way or the other, people have always voiced their heartaches and sorrows through song, just as they have expressed happiness and other emotions.

Many psalms are laments. They were honest expressions of how the people felt, and they were addressed to God. Those who lamented—whether it was an individual or a group—did not hide their feelings of sorrow or disappointment. They described their problems and told God how they felt about their difficulties.

152

It is in the Korahite's lamenting, as he described his situation, that we recognize the symptoms of his depression.

Crying

"Day and night I cry, and tears are my only food" (Ps. 42:3). A depressed person may either cry often or feel like crying often. When I was trying to help a friend determine if she was depressed, I asked, "Are you crying more than usual?" "Sobbing would be more like it," she responded. For the person who already cries easily, depression may mean what it did for my friend and for the psalmist, an increase in intensity. He cried day and night. For others it may mean crying for reasons that at other times wouldn't bother them.

Feeling Abandoned

"I say to God my Rock, 'Why have you forgotten me?'" (Ps. 42:9 NIV). Andrew Solomon, in his "atlas of depression," wrote that for many people depression is "an experience of being cast out by God or abandoned by Him." For most believers "this rage against God lifts as the depression lifts."[4] This sense of abandonment is a symptom of depression and not a fact.

Inner Turmoil

"You are God my stronghold. Why have you rejected me?" (Ps. 43:2 NIV). As we have already noted, opposing attitudes or feelings can and often do coexist in the heart and mind of a depressed person. The psalmist's lament contained expressions of gloom and distress and also elements of hope and confidence. He felt rejected by God, and yet he referred to him as his stronghold. He believed there was no place to worship God but in Jerusalem, yet he spoke to him right where he was. God wasn't present and yet he was. He felt as if God had sent all his troubles and yet he saw God as his rescuer.

Brooding about the Past

"My heart breaks when I remember the past" (Ps. 42:4). Sounds like another ruminator, doesn't he? Deeply dispirited, the psalmist contrasted past joys (when he led the pilgrim throng to the sanctuary) with the unhappy present. He longed for the return of his former happy conditions. He longed to return to Jerusalem where he could worship in the courts of the temple on the holy mountain. Memories kept jamming his head, coming back again and again, as he mulled over his past and tried to figure out why he was so disturbed. Over and over he asked, "Why?"[5] Why did he have to lose what was so precious to him? Why was he so unhappy?

Physical Pain

"My bones suffer mortal agony as my foes taunt me" (Ps. 42:10 NIV). The pain the psalmist felt was not just in his soul, he also felt it physically—his bones were suffering. He could be describing an actual physical ailment. Often depressed people suffer from physical complaints for which no medical explanation can be found. The psalmist could also be describing the pain of depression itself. It just hurt so much he felt as though someone were sticking knives into his bones.

Feeling Overwhelmed

"Deep calls to deep in the roar of your waterfalls; all your waves and breakers have swept over me" (Ps. 42:7 NIV). The psalmist used images of mighty waters to speak of his troubles. The roar of the waterfalls, the waves, and the breakers threatened to drown him. In other words, his troubles kept pouring forth, coming down on him in layer after layer, and overwhelming him.

Repeatedly the imagery of mighty waters is used to describe a powerful threat in Old Testament poetry. At times this threat may be literal waters, as Israel faced at the Red Sea or Jonah faced when tossed overboard during a violent storm. But in many cases "mighty waters" is a metaphor for some other threat, often a threat to life itself, such as it was for this psalmist.

It is not unusual for depressed people to use metaphors, even if they are not poets like the Korahite was. Descriptions of how they feel might be: "I'm in a tunnel and can't see the light at the end" or "I feel like I'm down in a well" or "I'm down in a valley." People who are depressed use these metaphors so repeatedly that, if I hear someone make any of these statements, I perk up and listen carefully to see what else is going on in his or her life. The person may be depressed.

Perhaps the Korahite chose the metaphor of water because it may have been at the source of the Jordan River where he prayed. No one knows where Mount Mizar was. Perhaps he was watching the waterfall, listening to the roar, watching cascade after cascade of water crash onto the rocks. Struck by the power, he wondered if anyone could survive beneath the falls. He wondered if he would survive, so he cried out to God for deliverance. He prayed an honest prayer, one from which we can learn.

The Instructive Psalm

Preceding Psalms 42 and 43 in both Hebrew manuscripts and the Greek Septuagint appear the words, "For the director of music. A *maskil* of the Sons of Korah." The word *maskil* also precedes several other psalms: 44–49, 84–85, 87, and 88. No one knows exactly what the word *maskil* means. Grappling with various possibilities, the Holman Christian Standard Bible says the verb form indicates the art of instructing. As these psalms were sung, they also taught, which shouldn't surprise us. Many persons learn truths about God from hymns they sing. From Psalms 42 and 43, we can learn ways to deal with depression.

Pray Honestly

The psalmist dealt with his loss by praying honestly. He poured out his soul (Ps. 42:4). He described his situation as he saw it, and he did not refrain from letting God know how unhappy he was. He even implied that God was responsible for his troubles: "All *your* waves and breakers have swept over me" (v. 7 NIV, italics added).

Pray the Psalms

When we have a hard time verbalizing what we are feeling, it can be helpful to pray the Psalms. When we are depressed, we may not always be able to articulate what's in our heart, but if we can identify with a psalmist, then we can pray the psalm. Many of the words and phrases used by psalmists are ones with which depressed persons can identify. Here's an example from one of David's psalms:

> Save me, O God,
>   for the waters have come up to my neck.
> I sink in the miry depths,
>   where there is no foothold.

> I have come into the deep waters;
> the floods engulf me.
> I am worn out calling for help;
> my throat is parched.
>
> Psalm 69:1–3 NIV

If you have trouble verbalizing your inner turmoil and asking God for help, you may want to look through the Psalms, find a description that sounds like how you feel, and make that psalm your prayer.

Write Freely

David wrote out his feelings in many psalms. For some people writing prayers is a meaningful and healing experience. In her book *Love Letters to God*, Lynn D. Morrissey told how writing her prayers to God transformed her life. As a young woman she was tormented by suicidal depression, and she drowned her despair in alcohol. She found it impossible, though, to verbalize her deep-seated fears and complex emotions. Her verbal "petitions to God just seemed to trail off into oblivion, unfinished, unexpressed."[6]

When a vengeful woman at work began telling lies about Lynn to get her fired, she vented her fears and frustrations on paper. The more she wrote, the better she felt. Without realizing what was happening, what she wrote turned into prayers to God, asking for his help. As she sought God through writing, he gave her calm at work, his peace replaced her depression, and his power gave her victory over drinking. She wrote, "I have found that there is something extraordinary about *writing* that frees me to express my emotions and thoughts like no other form of prayer can."[7]

157

Sing

The Psalms formed the songbooks of the Israelites and later of the early church. Today we sing many psalms as worship songs and choruses, including "As the deer panteth for the water, so my soul longeth after thee."

Singing gives us a tool for expressing our emotions and provides words to articulate what we may be feeling or thinking. As we express ourselves in this way, our mood improves. Making the effort to sing, even when we don't feel like it, unlocks feelings from within and lets them out, giving God room to work.

Talk to Your Soul

The psalmist addressed his lament to God, but he also talked to himself. Several times he said, "Why are you downcast, O my soul? Why so disturbed within me? Put your hope in God" (Ps. 42:5, 11; 43:5 NIV).

Other psalmists switched back and forth like this too, speaking to God and speaking to self. This switching should encourage those who have difficulty praying "organized" prayers. My label for organized praying is "composition"—a label that goes back to high school days when we wrote themes that had to have an introduction, body, and conclusion. Our prayers don't have to be compositions—continuous and organized—to be effective. In fact they may be more effective when we are more natural, even disjointed, and when we take time to pause and listen to God or talk to ourselves to stay on track, to dig deeper, or to remind ourselves of what is true.

The Korahite reminded himself of God's nature and his love, truths an overwhelmed person needs to remember. "By day the Lord directs his love, at night his song is with me" (42:8 NIV). As the psalmist released his emotions, remembered God's nature, talked to himself, poured out his soul, and prayed honestly, he grew in confidence. As bleak as things were, faith and hope broke through so that he prayed specifically and confidently. Lament gave way to petition. He asked God to vindicate him, defend him, and rescue him (43:1). He wanted his mighty, living God to show himself and he wanted relief!

Then his confidence wavered one more time—and that sometimes happens as we try to pray our way out of depression and sort out emotions. He questioned, "Why have you rejected me? Why must I go about mourning, oppressed by the enemy?" (v. 2). And then the honest praying, the pouring out of his soul, paid off. His mood totally changed.

Breakthrough

As the psalmist's confidence grew, it occurred to him that, if he was taking refuge in God, he could not be forsaken. An idea suddenly exploded in his head. *Light and truth—those are God's instruments!* He realized "that deceit is the enemy of light and injustice the enemy of truth. If, then, God will dispatch light and truth to his aid, they will guarantee him safe conduct to the holy hill, and to the dwelling place of God."[8]

Hope flared and burned within him. Ah, he might be able to go to the altar of God again. He would be able to praise him with his harp. God was his exceeding joy and delight (Ps. 43:4).

Is this the same man speaking? Yes it is, because the mighty Lord of the storm responded to an honest prayer. He reached down from on high to rescue a distressed man from the depths. The shepherd lifted up the cast-down sheep.

Did the psalmist actually make it back to the holy hill in Jerusalem to worship? We don't know, but we do know he believed in the possibility. He experienced spiritual victory. His mood changed, and hope was ignited. Like most biblical laments, his ended on a note of confidence and trust, because he had honestly prayed and given God room to do an inner work of grace.

The psalmist was so confident that he wondered how he could have been so despondent. How could there possibly have been faithlessness on his part (v. 5)? The dark circumstances of his life still surrounded him, but he could now see light and truth shining on the way before him. Because he sang the blues, he discovered that God was present and mighty in Jordan as well as in Jerusalem.

Replay and Reflect

What is your worship preference? What would be your reaction if you were forced to worship in another manner?

Was the question "Why am I so depressed?" a good one or a poor one for the psalmist to ask himself?

What metaphor would you use to describe life?

What metaphor would you use to describe a down time?

If you have trouble verbalizing your prayers, what options do you have to express yourself to God?

What specifically do you expect from God when you pray?

11

⊰| Paul |⊱

When the Pressure Is Keen

The burdens laid upon us were so great
and so heavy that we gave up all hope.

2 CORINTHIANS 1:8

My friendship with Geneva (not her real name) started a few months before my second book on depression was published. We were serving on a board together. I appreciated her candid comments in the board meetings and was impressed by her unflappability. When she asked me to lunch, I was pleased because I wanted to get to know her.

Over salad, I learned about her job as a human resource director, about her family, and about her other community activities. The list was long!

She was nice to ask about my work too, so I told her about the soon-to-be-released book. She said, "I want a copy when it comes out." I assumed she was just being polite, so when the book was published, I didn't give her one. But after several months she asked for a copy. She read it and told me it was helpful. *Helpful?* I looked at her quizzically. She said, "I'm bipolar and I take lithium." That's all. She didn't elaborate or speak of her depression again. As our friendship grew, I learned she was a stoic person who didn't talk much about herself or her feelings.

The apostle Paul was the same way. He did not reveal his feelings as did Jeremiah, Elijah, Jonah, Job, and the Korahite psalmist. This doesn't mean he had nothing to complain about. On the contrary, his life was full of challenges:

He was often troubled and sometimes in doubt.

He had enemies.

He endured hardships and difficulties.

He was beaten, jailed, and mobbed.

He was overworked, and, at times, went without sleep, food, shelter, and clothing.

He spent time in jail.

He was mistreated, called a liar, punished, saddened, and poor.

Five times he was flogged.

Three times he was beaten with rods.

Once he was stoned.

He knew hunger and cold, and three times he was shipwrecked.

He encountered dangers in the cities, dangers in the wilds, dangers on the high seas, dangers from robbers, false friends, fellow Jews, and Gentiles.

At times he was near death.

He experienced a thorn in the flesh and unanswered prayer.

His apostleship was questioned and criticized.

He carried within him the pressure of his concern for all the churches.

His heart was intertwined with others so that if someone was weak, then he felt weak too. When someone was led into sin, he was filled with distress.[1]

As you can see, his life was filled with fodder for depression. Yet Paul seldom uttered a discouraging word. He wrote little about himself and his personal struggles. He wasn't the type to parade his sufferings, so it would be easy to assume that Paul never struggled with depression. That wouldn't be quite right, though, because on three occasions, it appears that he did: when he was in Asia, when he was worried about relationships, and when he was on his way to Rome.

The Asian Mystery

When Paul wrote his second letter to the Corinthians, he had just been in Ephesus, one of the leading cities of Asia. He mentioned experiencing hardships there. He said, "We were under great pressure, far beyond our ability to endure, so that we despaired even of life. Indeed, in our hearts we felt the sentence of death" (2 Cor. 1:8–9 NIV).

The distress Paul experienced in Asia weighed him down. The load was just too heavy to carry, and he couldn't see an escape. He was at the end of his rope and so crushed by the experience that dying seemed imminent. It was useless to go on living.

What happened in Asia to cause him to feel this way? No one knows for sure. It could have been any of a number of things considering the situation in Ephesus.

Rioting

Paul stopped briefly in Ephesus on his second missionary journey (Acts 18:19), and then he went back for a three-year stay on his third journey, right before he wrote this letter to the Corinthians.

He had started out speaking in the synagogue, as was his usual custom when he arrived in a city with a synagogue. As usual, there was bitter opposition to his preaching, so after three months Paul left the synagogue and taught in the hall of Tyrannus. Many lives were changed through Paul's teachings. There were miracles, and a deathblow was struck to superstition, but a strong backlash occurred. With extreme outrage, many of the people rioted against Paul. After the uproar died down, Paul left and continued on his journey. Had the backlash against him been the pressure that caused him to despair of life?

Church Problems

Could something involving the church in Ephesus have caused his despair? Later on this same journey, Paul was near Ephesus again and could have easily returned there, but he didn't. Instead, he asked the Ephesian elders to meet him at Miletus. In speaking with them, he mentioned the hard times he experienced with them, "because of the plots of some Jews" (Acts 20:19). He also warned them about fierce wolves that would come among them, stirring up the flock and causing problems. Maybe he had already encountered some of those wolves and could still feel their teeth marks when he wrote to the Corinthians.

Beasts

In an earlier letter to the Corinthians, when talking about perils he faced, he mentioned fighting beasts in Ephesus (1 Cor. 15:32). Legend had it that he actually fought lions in an arena there, but that is unlikely because he was a Roman citizen, and no Roman citizen could be made to fight in an arena. He was probably referring to people who treated him as savagely as wild beasts. You may know some people you think of as beasts!

How Paul Recovered

Whether it was because of the rioting, church problems, or beasts, the atmosphere at Ephesus was so intense and heavy that Paul lost hope and he believed he would die—two clear signs he was depressed. But he didn't stay depressed, and his letter suggests two reasons for this.

Turning Negatives into Positives

Paul did not linger in depression and did not get stuck in the darkness, because he fanned his hope by continually voicing confidence in God. Paul saw purpose in the Asian experience. He said, "*But* this happened that we might not rely on ourselves but on God" (2 Cor. 1:9 NIV, italics added). Finding himself out of his own strength, he was forced to depend on God for deliverance, and he saw this as a good thing. God was growing him.

165

Frequently Paul added a "but" or a "yet" to his narratives, giving a positive twist to difficulties he experienced:

> "We are often troubled, *but* not crushed; sometimes in doubt, *but* never in despair; there are many enemies, *but* we are never without a friend; and though badly hurt at times, we are not destroyed" (4:8–9, italics added).

> "We are treated as liars, *yet* we speak the truth; as unknown, *yet* we are known by all; as though we were dead, *but*, as you see, we live on. Although punished, we are not killed; although saddened, we are always glad; we seem poor, *but* we make many people rich; we seem to have nothing, *yet* we really possess everything" (6:8–10, italics added).

By countering each negative with a positive, Paul was using a technique cognitive therapists use with their depressed clients. They challenge them to restate, rewrite, or refute their thoughts, and when they do, their feelings change. Paul didn't know anything about cognitive therapy, but he knew the importance of changing one's thinking. In this same letter to the Corinthians, he said, "We take every thought captive and make it obey Christ" (10:5).

This is a practice we can develop. As we verbalize our difficulties, we can add a "but" or a "yet" that acknowledges what Jesus can do in our situation. Or on paper we can write down each negative thought and write a positive rebuttal to each. Whether verbal or written, our hope level will rise and we will grow in confidence, as Paul did, that God will deliver us (1:10).

Prayer Support

Paul also counted on the prayer support of others, which is why he mentioned this Asian incident to the Corinthians.

He wrote, "From such terrible dangers of death [God] saved us, and will save us; and we have placed our hope in him that he will save us again, as you help us by means of your prayers for us" (2 Cor. 1:10–11). Theirs was a partnership in ministry as they helped and encouraged each other. For that reason Paul wanted them also to share the joy of seeing God's answer (v. 11). If he didn't mention a need for prayer, then they would not have the experience of delighting in God's answer.

This is another piece of evidence pointing to Paul's positive outlook, always looking for God to answer. There was no "if" in his mind. He believed that God would answer in such a tangible way that the Corinthians could recognize the answer along with him. They could rejoice together!

By mentioning his depression and asking for prayer, he was saying to the Corinthians, "Share my life, my struggles, my faith, and my joy, because I value our relationship." He needed to say something like this because at the time, their relationship was shaky.

The Anxious Letter Writer

An earlier visit with the Corinthians had not gone well. Paul was pained by how they treated him, by what they said about him, and by how things were going in the church at Corinth. Should he ignore the tension and move on? Should he visit them again? Or should he write them? Another visit might be too painful for them, so Paul wrote a letter. It was a stern letter but it needed to be, if he was to wake them up regarding their behavior. Writing the letter wasn't easy for Paul. He wrote it "out of great distress and anguish of heart and with many tears" (2 Cor. 2:4 NIV). Paul sent the letter by Titus, a young friend whom he was mentoring.

Paul instructed Titus to take this letter to Corinth and let him know what happened.

Once you have done something like this—confronted someone about his or her actions, whether it is a subordinate at work, an adult child, or a fellow Christian, the time that follows can be an anxious one. After Titus was on his way, Paul began worrying. Would Titus make it? How would the Corinthians receive him? Earlier when Paul had sent a letter by Timothy, he had been rebuffed. Would Titus get the same treatment? Would they give him a hard time? Would they even receive the letter? Should he have written it? How would they feel about a stern letter? Would this letter do further damage to his relationship with Corinthian believers or improve it? Would they be willing to make any changes? Would Titus make it back okay?

Full of concerns, Paul became impatient for Titus to return. Paul left Ephesus where he wrote the stern letter and went to Troas hoping to meet Titus there. While he waited, he preached and received the kind of reception that would usually make him want to stick around, but he was deeply worried because he could not find Titus. So he said "good-bye to the people there and went on to Macedonia" (v. 13).

By the time he got to Macedonia, his anxiety had snowballed, making a perfect breeding ground for depression. As Paul described it, "When we came into Macedonia our flesh had no rest, but we were afflicted on every side; conflicts without, fears within" (7:5 NASB). Outwardly harassed and inwardly distressed, he couldn't rest, and his whole body was full of tension. The fighting without could have been opposition from pagan foes in Macedonia or troubles in the church there—trouble seemed to follow Paul! Within were the fears and haunting anxiety concerning the situation at Corinth. The fear of an adverse report gnawed at him, and gloom prevailed.

When Titus arrived safe and sound, he had good news! He said the situation at Corinth had improved immensely, and the Corinthian believers were determined to do better. They had repented of their hard feelings (v. 9) and felt kindly toward him and toward Paul (v. 7).

With Titus's heartening report, Paul's depression lifted. It simply dissipated, which can happen with some depressions. The right kind of sunshine can suddenly light up the darkness. This is in contrast to heavier or more complicated depressions that we must walk out of, taking a step here and a step there, getting a little better day by day. Some depressions can be readily resolved, as was Paul's with good news. Naturally, Paul credited God for rescuing him.

He wrote, "But God, who comforts the depressed, comforted us by the coming of Titus; and not only by his coming, but also by the comfort with which he was comforted in you, as he reported to us your longing, your mourning, your zeal for me; so that I rejoiced even more" (vv. 6–7 NASB). What a joy and a relief the news from Corinth was!

It would be easy to take a glib approach to Paul's pain and say, "Everything worked out, so Paul should have had more faith. He didn't need to worry." People who take this approach with those who are depressed minimize their pain; they don't see the variables involved. Often Paul's plans didn't work out. He had frequent people problems, and much was at stake for the future of his ministry and the church at Corinth if he ignored the tension between them. To minimize his pain is not to fully appreciate what he was experiencing and to learn from this incident.

Taking a firm stand, such as Paul did by writing a stern letter and sending it to Corinth, is often followed by a period in which even strong people are vulnerable to fears, anxieties, and worry. It seems to be part of the challenge of the situation. Usually when we make a weighty decision that involves risk, we are unable to conclude, "Well, that takes care of that" and never give it another thought. The decision does not end the challenge. There's always the "follow-through," the repercussions that result from doing God's will. Usually the feeling of vulnerability will fade, but sometimes when the stakes are high, it can be a time of anxiety and even depression as it was for Paul. The marvel is that Paul hung on, continuing to minister to others and continuing to focus on what God called him to do.

Paul is also to be commended because he wrote the stern letter. To have not taken this step would have let the situation fester and go unresolved, ultimately making it even harder to correct, perhaps even impossible. How that would have grieved Paul and weighed on his heart and mind! How that would have been detrimental to his ministry in Corinth and the surrounding province of Achaia! Quite possibly by taking this step, he warded off more serious depression—the kind that would have been really hard to heal.

In his relief and joy, Paul saw God at work. He said, "But God, who comforts the depressed, comforted us" (v. 6 NASB). God had not forgotten him! God cared for his servant! This is something we should all keep in mind. When we are struggling, we should never discount the possibility that God may shine a light in the darkness.

Shipwrecked

When Paul completed this third missionary tour, he was falsely accused and arrested by the Jews in Jerusalem. The

Roman commander in charge wanted to find out exactly why the Jews were so angry with Paul, so he took him before their supreme court. What Paul said before the court divided the members. "The argument became so violent that the commander was afraid that Paul would be torn to pieces. So he ordered his soldiers to go down into the group, get Paul away from them, and take him into the fort" (Acts 23:10).

"That night the Lord stood by Paul and said, 'Don't be afraid! You have given your witness for me here in Jerusalem, and you must also do the same in Rome'" (v. 11).

The next day forty Jews vowed to kill Paul. When the commander heard this, he whisked Paul off to Caesarea, where the Judean governor, Felix, kept Paul under guard. When Festus replaced Felix, he wanted to settle Paul's case by taking Paul back to Jerusalem. Although two years had passed, Paul's memories of what happened in Jerusalem were still fresh in his mind. He knew he wouldn't get a fair trial there, so he claimed his rights as a Roman citizen. He said, "I appeal to Caesar."

"Very well," said Festus. "You have appealed to Caesar, so to Caesar you must go."

Accompanied by a Roman centurion and his friends Luke and Aristarchus, Paul was taken as a prisoner to Rome to stand trial before Caesar. Now Paul, with his penchant for turning a negative into a positive, saw this as the way to get to Rome to further the gospel. Unfortunately, the vessel he was traveling on ran into strong winds and stormy weather.

Never one to withhold his opinion, Paul said to the crew, "'Men, I can see that our voyage is going to be disastrous and bring great loss to ship and cargo, and to our own lives also.' But the centurion, instead of listening to what Paul said, followed the advice of the pilot and of the owner of the ship" (27:10–11 NIV).

The crew labored exceedingly to save the ship in the storm, even throwing part of the ship's equipment overboard. As the violent storm continued, everyone became frightened. Luke described the depression that gripped them: "For many days we could not see the sun or the stars, and the wind kept on blowing very hard. We finally gave up all hope of being saved" (v. 20).

These words weren't Paul's, so perhaps I shouldn't conclude he was depressed by the stormy conditions, yet if he wasn't, why did he wait so long before encouraging the others? They had gone a long time without food before Paul said, "I beg you, take courage! Not one of you will lose your life; only the ship will be lost" (v. 22).

From this point on, Paul was confident and hopeful. He instructed those on board about what to do and reassured them no lives would be lost. He was calm, dignified, and direct. What happened to cause the change? The God who comforts the depressed sent him a message.

Hearing from God

No doubt Paul was affected by the storm as the others were. Endless days and nights of torrential rain can get the best of anyone, especially someone on a shaky ship that might sink at any time. Plus Paul had other concerns, such as getting his case settled and carrying the gospel to Rome. What happened to the reassuring words the Lord gave him after the chaos in the court in Jerusalem? Had he not heard God correctly? Was God going to disappoint him? How could he encourage others when he himself was so discouraged?

And then everything changed. An angel appeared and said, "Do not be afraid, Paul. You must stand trial before Caesar; and God has graciously given you the lives of all who sail with you" (Acts 27:24 NIV).

After the angel's appearance, Paul became the person in charge. With his depression gone, he directed the people on board about what to do. He reassured them that they would survive, and they did. No lives were lost.

This incident of depression is different from the others we have studied. From those, we learned what *we could do* to get over depression, but in this shipwreck incident, the Bible doesn't show us that Paul did anything to resolve his depression. God, at his own initiative, acted to resolve Paul's depression by sending a heavenly messenger.

Of course, Paul may have been doing something. He may have been below deck praying, pleading with God to rescue them as the storm battered the ship, but if he was, neither he nor Luke tells us.

What we do know—and what I hope will be heartening to you—is that God saw his plight and responded in a supernatural way. He had a purpose for Paul's life, and he had plans for him to share the gospel in Rome. He was not going to abandon Paul.

This occasion wasn't the only time God ministered to Paul like this. Paul experienced several supernatural manifestations in the way of visions and revelations from the Lord.[2] Most came at critical times in his life. None, as far as I can tell, came because Paul initiated them or took *specific* steps to get God to respond in a certain way. They came because God loved Paul and had a purpose for his life, and he does for us too. This is a factor we never want to forget when we are struggling with depression.

The God Factor

As we have seen in this book, effort is very important in overcoming depression, but, at the same time, we don't want to discount the possibility of God's acting on our behalf. It's a hope to hold on to. I mention this because the pessimistic nature of depression works against entertaining the possibility. The symptom of feeling estranged from God that some depressed people experience can keep them from believing that he would care enough to do anything. And when we exert effort to get well, we may begin to think, *It's all up to me. If I don't work hard, I will never find relief.* But to think like that is to leave God out of the picture.

I can't tell you for sure what God will do, but from this study and from my own experience, I can tell you that he will act. You may hear him in someone's prayers, he may reassure you through the words of a good friend or a counselor, or he may give you a vision or a revelation or send an angel to visit you. He may be looking out for you without your even realizing it. More than ten years after my struggle, I discovered one important way he was looking out for me.

A woman at church asked me, "Who would you recommend for a doctor who will diagnose depression?" This is a genuine concern for many people, as depression is hard to diagnose because of its many symptoms and various disguises. The woman explained that she was certain her adult daughter was depressed, but none of the three doctors she had been to for her physical symptoms spotted it. The daughter needed help and yet she was resisting her mother's suggestion that she might be depressed. She needed someone with medical authority to confirm it.

I said, "I'm sorry, I don't know anyone in this area."

She said, "Well, who diagnosed yours?"

As I explained to her that we lived in another state when I was depressed, a warm glow enveloped me—the kind of warmth you experience when you know in a tangible way that God loves you. I suddenly realized how fortunate I was to have had a doctor who diagnosed my depression. When I went to see him, I was certain I had other terrible things wrong with me. He let me have my way for a while, and then he told me I was depressed. I said I wasn't, and he insisted that I was. He listened to all my arguments, and then said, "Your denial is a classic symptom." That's when I surrendered and admitted I was depressed.

This same doctor made an appointment for me to see a psychiatrist before I left his office. He knew that I would probably not have done it on my own, and he was right! I would have gone home and tried to handle it all on my own, which I was beyond doing. I needed professional help. As it was, when I walked out of the doctor's office, I was taking the first few steps toward recovery.

God was there all the time even when I thought he wasn't. I was a blessed woman who had a doctor who could spot depression. As he did for Paul, God turned my misery into ministry because he loves me and has a purpose for my life. Who knows? He may be acting on your behalf right now. There's always that possibility when you worship "the God who comforts the depressed" (2 Cor. 7:6 NASB).

Replay and Reflect

What is the greatest pressure you're now facing?

Why do you think Paul talked so little about his struggles, even though he had so many?

What are some ways you can take every thought captive?

Why should you ask for the prayer support of others?

How can the "follow-through" of a decision be part of the challenge?

Why would God send Paul a heavenly messenger if he hadn't prayed for one?

12

Treasures in the Darkness

We've been in good company as we've walked with biblical saints through their valleys. We rubbed elbows with leaders like Moses and Saul, men who could inspire and motivate others to follow. We fell in step with some impeccably good people, such as Job and Paul. We saw into the hearts of two courageous women, Naomi and Hannah, who loved fiercely and openly. We caught a glimpse of the working of a wise man's mind and heard the panting of a devoted worshiper. We observed the forthrightness of God's spokespersons—Jeremiah, Elijah, and Jonah—who struggled with what God called them to do. Still, they knew for certain that he had called, so they followed. All were strong individuals; no weaklings among these people! Yet for a time, each walked through the valley of depression. What caused their descent varied from catastrophic loss to bad weather and included being puzzled over what God was doing or not doing.

Their ascent out of depression varied as well. Most of these saints emerged from their low places. They did indeed march again! And we can too. We can walk out of the valleys where saints sometimes go, particularly if we are willing to learn.

Lessons from the Saints

Not every saint that we've studied used the same approach to recovery, and God didn't respond to each of them in the same way. From both their efforts and God's responses, however, we have learned ways we can help ourselves.

Recognize Our Load Limits

We all have a limit to what we can handle and endure. Some have higher limits than others, but there's a point for all of us when our load is too heavy. If we're in a valley now, we may be there because we need a rest, whether our heavy load is emotional, mental, spiritual, physical, or all four combined! If we are not currently in a valley, we can think about our lives and evaluate our load. Is it getting close to our limit? If it is, now is the time to find ways to reduce our load.

Honest Praying

At times this has felt like a book on prayer. We learned several ways to deal prayerfully with depression, but the most prevalent way was honest prayer. When the saints prayed honestly, they did not hold back their thoughts or emotions as they verbalized their inner turmoil and sought relief. God didn't always respond in the same way to each one, but he always responded. Your hurt and your pain may be signaling you that it is time for you to be honest. It is time to cast *all* your cares on God (1 Peter 5:7).

Questions

Often God used questions to encourage the saints to vent and to get them to think. Are we willing to *answer* questions? The questions may come from friends, counselors, associates, clergy, and God, as well as from this book (at the end of each chapter). Our tendency, when we are depressed, is not to answer. We don't want to be confronted; we don't want anyone to challenge our watertight reasons for being depressed. But our study of the saints shows us that we will march with keener insight and firmer steps if we are willing to answer questions.

Look for Alternatives

When our situation looks hopeless, and we can't see any alternatives, we may need to *ask* questions. We can talk to friends, family members, clergy, or a counselor about our dilemma, asking, Am I missing something here? Can you see anything I can do that would make a difference in my situation?

While this step takes courage, it is beneficial. You may be like Moses who couldn't see that sharing the load was the solution to his dilemma. Seeing possibilities raises hope. Even if you don't like the alternatives, at least you realize there *is* something you can do.

Take Action

We can take action, even if it is a small step. If Moses hadn't followed God's directions and divided up his responsibilities, he would not have walked out of the valley. He had to take a step to begin his road to recovery.

When Naomi concocted a plan, her recovery started. It broke up her ruminating about the past and gave her something to focus on.

Solomon's story reminded us of the importance of taking steps, to keep walking in the light of what we know is true, not what we feel is true.

Taking action, whether it is one step or several, engages momentum, giving us a forward thrust and a push upward, which is important because leaving the valley is an uphill climb.

Change Our Thinking

Several of our saints didn't quite have their situation estimated correctly. Their comments revealed their erroneous thinking, which had to change if they were to get well. I can't begin to imagine what my life would be like today if I hadn't learned to recognize my faulty thinking patterns. I am so much happier than I would have been otherwise. Challenging my thinking cleared out the cobwebs, changed my perspective, and enhanced my sense of well-being. I became a huge fan of *Feeling Good: The New Mood Therapy* by David Burns,[1] a book that helps you recognize your distorted thinking and gives you ways to change your thinking. In workshops on depression, I hold it up and say, "Outside of the Bible, this is the best self-help book there is." Realistically I know that not all depressed people need this kind of help, but the change in my own life has been so great, I can't help but recommend this book. This change in my thinking—and consequently my happiness level—is one reason, as I said in the introduction, "I count depression as one of the best things to ever happen to me."

Consider Our Associates

What kind of friends do you have? Do you have friends like Job's who had simplistic, rigid explanations for his losses, or do you have friends like those of Naomi and Paul? Ruth rolled up her shirtsleeves and found a way to provide for Naomi and herself. Titus, Luke, and Aristarchus traveled with Paul, ministered to his needs, and helped him through difficult situations.

As hard as it may be, if we want to get over being depressed, we may have to withdraw from relationships that contribute to our pessimism and negativity. Instead, we need to seek out friends who will be understanding and supportive. And if we don't already have friends like this, then now is the time to begin building positive relationships, because we all need friends to help us through the twists and turns of life—whether we go through depression or some other difficulty. God never meant for us to handle life alone.

A Willingness to Let Go

We may need to let go of the past, the grief, the fears, the disgruntlement. They are baggage that weighs us down. We may even have to give up our right to know the reasons for our sufferings. We could hold out and keep insisting on our right to feel the way we do, while life is passing us by. On this side of eternity we may never know the reasons for our sufferings, but we do know that there is a God who can be trusted. And even when we are not aware of it, he is working, and you will discover as I did that God was there all the time you were depressed. You were not alone in the valley.

As we learn these lessons, we are reminded over and over that life is not a level plateau. There are ups and downs, dips and turns. There are peaks and there are valleys. For our own well-being, it is important to look at our times in the valleys. Not all believers are willing to do that.

Always on the Sunny Side

Many believers want to live life on the peaks where everything is bright and sunny, believing that, if you follow Christ, this is where life should be lived. They resist having anything to do with dark and gray areas, assuming that when you are in sync with God's will, everything goes well and the sun should be shining.

But walking in the valley, whether our own or with someone else, gives us the opportunity to wrestle with truths others may take for granted. It gives us a chance to think about what we really believe, maybe even discarding some of our incorrect theology and expanding our knowledge of God. And when you have wrestled with your beliefs in the darkness and had your thinking challenged, solid truth emerges, truth you can hold on to. Your strong convictions can even inspire others.

Martin Luther believed that "intense upheavals of the spirit" were necessary for just this kind of learning. For example, he said that others may talk about hope but not know what that really means or how essential it is to the human spirit, unless they have struggled with hopelessness. In his deepest depression, Luther wrote: "A mighty fortress is our God, a bulwark never failing," and we feel the power of his convictions every time we sing it.

I'm not suggesting a believer should deliberately entertain darkness just to learn. What I'm saying is that we can find treasures in the darkness. There is no place we can go that God is not there or where he refuses to work with us.

What treasures could God have for you in the darkness? Does God have a new song for you to sing? Or will you cling to the blues?

I stopped singing the blues when I believed once again that God had a purpose for my life. The deeper lesson that I learned—the one that stays with me—is the knowledge that I cannot function without this sense of purpose. When those puzzling incidents come along in life that make me question God's realness or make me want to throw up my hands in despair, I don't pause there for long. I know I have to believe in God to survive, and I want to make the most of the life he has given me.

When one of my sons was struggling spiritually, he asked, "Mother, how do you know God is real?"

I said, "I could quote Bible verses to try to convince you of God's realness. I could give you the arguments of great theologians, but that's not how I know. I have tried living life with God and without him. I've learned I can't live without him." That I learned in the darkness.

I need a purpose to live, a purpose with eternal significance. This knowledge fortifies me. It is my still small voice.

This knowledge is my bronze wall.

It is my bulwark never failing.

It keeps me marching.

That's why today I'm still a born-again, Bible-believing, faith-teaching, regular pray-er. The depression doesn't stay with us forever, but what we learn in the darkness does.

Notes

Introduction

1. Andrew Solomon, *The Noonday Demon: An Atlas of Depression* (New York: Scribner, 2001), 285.

2. Leslie D. Weatherhead, *Prescription for Anxiety* (Nashville: Abingdon, 1956), 30–31.

Chapter 2 Naomi

1. G. Ernest Wright, *Great People of the Bible and How They Lived* (1974; reprint, Pleasantville, NY: Reader's Digest Association, 1979), 126.

2. Virginia Stem Owens, *Daughters of Eve* (Colorado Springs: NavPress, 1995), 48.

3. Roland H. Bainton, *Here I Stand: A Life of Martin Luther* (Nashville: Abingdon-Cokesbury, 1950), 363.

Chapter 3 Job

1. *The Interpreter's Bible*, vol. 3 (Nashville: Abingdon, 1954), 925.

2. John White, *The Masks of Melancholy: A Christian Physician Looks at Depression and Suicide* (Downers Grove, IL: InterVarsity, 1982), 15–17.

Chapter 4 Hannah

1. Michael Perry, "Drought Casts Suicide Shadow over Rural Australia," Reuters, June 6, 2005.

2. *The Interpreter's Bible*, vol. 2, 877.

3. Ibid., 879.

Chapter 6 Elijah

1. Archibald D. Hart, *Coping with Depression in the Ministry and Other Helping Professions* (Waco, TX: Word, 1984), 19.

Chapter 7 Jeremiah

1. See Jeremiah 11:18–12:4; 15:10–21; 17:12–18; 18:18–23; 20:7–18.

2. Martin E. P. Seligman, *What You Can Change and What You Can't* (New York: Fawcett Columbine, 1993), 95.

3. Clyde T. Francisco, *Studies in Jeremiah* (Nashville: Convention Press, 1961), 78–79.

4. After chapter 20 the personal whining ceases.

Chapter 8 Jonah

1. *The Interpreter's Bible*, vol. 6, 892.

2. James R. Edwards, *The Divine Intruder* (Colorado Springs: NavPress, 2000), 103.

3. David A. Seamands, *Healing for Damaged Emotions* (Wheaton, IL: Victor, 1985), 125.

Chapter 9 Solomon

1. Solomon, *The Noonday Demon*, 130.

2. Traditionally, authorship of Ecclesiastes has been attributed to Solomon, though no writer is named in the book. The author calls himself by the Hebrew name Koheleth, which is variously translated as "the Preacher," "the Philosopher," or "the Teacher." Regardless whether Koheleth was Solomon, he had lived a Solomon-like life. He was a son of David (1:1) and a king in Jerusalem (1:1, 12, 16) who had experienced many pleasures, much wealth, and worldy success. Consequently, what we can learn from this man is the same whether the author was Solomon or someone else.

3. *The Interpreter's Bible*, vol. 5, 5.

4. Ellen E. Davis, *Proverbs, Ecclesiastes, and the Song of Songs* (Louisville, KY: Westminster John Knox Press, 2000), 171.

5. David Burns, *Feeling Good: The New Mood Therapy* (New York: The New American Library, 1980), 37.

6. I'm grateful to Dr. William R. Parker and Elaine St. Johns, authors of *Prayer Can Change Your Life* (New York: Simon and Schuster, 1957), for helping me see how to pray about changing my will.

Chapter 10 A Psalmist

1. *The Interpreter's Bible*, vol. 4, 221.

2. Phillip Keller, *A Shepherd Looks at Psalm 23* (Minneapolis: World Wide Publications, 1970), 60.

3. Ibid., 61–62.

4. Solomon, *The Noonday Demon*, 130.

5. In Psalms 42 and 43, the word *why* occurs nine or ten times, depending on which version you read.

6. Lynn D. Morrissey, *Love Letters to God* (Sisters, OR: Multnomah, 2004), 6.

7. Ibid., 7.

8. *The Interpreter's Bible*, vol. 4, 226.

Chapter 11 Paul

1. This list of Paul's difficulties is based on 2 Corinthians 4:8–9; 6:4–5, 8–10; and 11:23–29.

2. Specific times in which Paul received supernatural manifestations are in these Bible passages: Acts 9; 16:9; 18:9; 22:17; 23:11; 27; 2 Cor. 12:1–6.

Chapter 12 Treasures in the Darkness

1. Burns, *Feeling Good: The New Mood Therapy.*

Bibliography

Bainton, Roland H. *Here I Stand: A Life of Martin Luther.* Nashville: Abingdon-Cokesbury, 1950.

Burns, David. *Feeling Good: The New Mood Therapy.* New York: The New American Library, 1980.

Claypool, John. *Glad Reunion: Meeting Ourselves in the Lives of Bible Men and Women.* Waco, TX: Word, 1985.

Davis, Ellen E. *Proverbs, Ecclesiastes, and the Song of Songs.* Louisville, KY: Westminster John Knox, 2000.

Edwards, James R. *The Divine Intruder.* Colorado Springs: NavPress, 2000.

Francisco, Clyde T. *Studies in Jeremiah.* Nashville: Convention Press, 1961.

Hart, Archibald D. *Coping with Depression in the Ministry and Other Helping Professions.* Waco, TX: Word, 1984.

House, Paul R. *Old Testament Survey.* Nashville: Broadman, 1992.

The Interpreter's Bible. Vols. 2, 3, 4, 6. Nashville: Abingdon, 1953, 1954, 1955, 1956.

Keil, C. F. *Commentary on the Old Testament Minor Prophets.* Vol. X. Grand Rapids: Eerdmans.

Keller, Phillip. *A Shepherd Looks at Psalm 23.* Minneapolis: World Wide Publications, 1970.

Morrissey, Lynn D. *Love Letters to God*. Sisters, OR: Multnomah, 2004.

Owens, Virginia Stem. *Daughters of Eve*. Colorado Springs: NavPress, 1995.

Perry, Michael. "Drought Casts Suicide Shadow over Rural Australia." Reuters, June 6, 2005.

Poinsett, Brenda. *Understanding a Woman's Depression*. Carol Stream, IL: Tyndale, 1984.

————. *Why Do I Feel This Way? What Every Woman Needs to Know about Depression*. Colorado Springs: NavPress, 1996.

Radius, Marianne. *Two Spies on a Rooftop*. Grand Rapids: Baker, 1968.

Seamands, David A. *Healing for Damaged Emotions*. Wheaton, IL: Victor, 1985.

Seligman, Martin E. P. *What You Can Change and What You Can't*. New York: Fawcett Columbine, 1993.

Solomon, Andrew. *The Noonday Demon: An Atlas of Depression*. New York: Scribner, 2001.

Stevens, William W. *A Guide for Old Testament Study*. Nashville: Broadman, 1974.

Weatherhead, Leslie D. *Prescription for Anxiety*. Nashville: Abingdon, 1956.

White, John. *The Masks of Melancholy: A Christian Physician Looks at Depression and Suicide*. Downers Grove, IL: InterVarsity, 1982.

Wirt, Sherwood Eliot. *A Thirst for God: Reflections on the Forty-second and Forty-third Psalms*. 1980. Reprint, Minneapolis: World Wide Publications, 1989.

Wold, Margaret. *Women of Faith and Spirit: Profiles of Fifteen Biblical Witnesses*. Minneapolis: Augsburg, 1987.

Wright, G. Ernest. *Great People of the Bible and How They Lived*. 1974. Reprint, Pleasantville, NY: Reader's Digest Association, 1979.

Brenda Poinsett is the author of twelve books and numerous articles in publications such as *Today's Christian Woman*, *Discipleship Journal*, *Pray*, and *Hearts at Home*. Brenda holds a B.S. from Southern Illinois University and an M.R.E. from Southwestern Baptist Theological Seminary. She speaks at conferences and seminars across the country and lives in Union, Missouri.